Behind Closed Doors

MEMOIRS OF MOTHERHOOD, MARRIAGE AND MENTAL HEALTH

LAURA LAWRENCE

Behind Closed Doors: Memoirs of Motherhood, Marriage and Mental Health

ISBN 978-1-7775371-5-9 (softcover)
ISBN: 978-1-7775371-6-6 (hardcover)
ISBN: 978-1-7775371-7-3 (ebook)

Love Bug Books
Laura Lawrence
www.lauralawrence.ca
Editor: Lisa K. Boehm
Book Cover & Interior Design: STOKE Publishing

To my mother, Catherine - you were right, about everything. I thank God for you every day, my root and my anchor.

To my daughter, Sydney - from the moment they placed us heart-to-heart, I knew I would love you forever. I just never knew how damn hard motherhood would be. I promise you, every shade of it, even the darkest ones, has been worth being your mama.

Contents

Preface

The *heart work* women do on this planet is sacred. I have felt this deep in my soul since I was just a young girl, watching and learning from the matriarchs in my own family and community. This *heart work* is raw, real and vulnerable - just like the hearts of the women who have courageously shared their stories in this book. I do not take the responsibility of being the one to share their stories lightly. I have held them in my hands and heart delicately, and I hope you will too. Parts of my own story are woven in the midst of these thirteen memoirs. I am who I am today because of all of the women who have shared even just a small piece of themselves with me over the last ten years of my self-discovery and journey back from the *darkness* after life threw me an unexpected curve ball. Inside these memoirs are tender subjects that may evoke deep emotion and trigger some of your own trauma. Please be gentle with yourself, and reach out for help to a loved one or professional if you are in need.

I am forever grateful to the thirteen women who sat heart-to-heart with me to bring this collection of memoirs to you. These heart-to-heart conversations took place on Treaty 6 land, also known as the central part of Saskatchewan. It is the home of the Cree, Saulteaux, Dakota, Lakota, and Dené Nations and the homeland of the Métis People. I am committed to acknowledging my privilege on this lifelong journey of both learning and unlearning in the spirit of truth and reconciliation.

Prologue

TIRED MOTHER

"Do you not like me, Mama?" a tiny voice whispered. My empathetic 3-year-old snuggled up close to me one morning watching the tears slide down my freckled-face cheeks. I was a hot mess that week; a complete emotional disaster and he could feel every single bit of it.

"No buddy, I love you very much. Mama is just sad and having a few bad days."

We were 15 months into the unprecedented Covid-19 pandemic, and as a self-employed entrepreneur who craved connection and social time, trying to balance running a household with four kids between the ages of 3 and 16 with my husband, I was barely managing to keep my head above water.

"Well, please don't get angry at my brother, Mama."

Cue more tears and the *mom guilt*: always the *mom guilt*. It was a week of non-stop emotional meltdowns, headaches, intense body pain, and overwhelm in every direction I looked. My house, my fridge, my office, my car - everything was a complete disaster. My outside world was very much a direct reflection of the turmoil that was going on inside of my head. I was on a subconscious mission to do some emotional damage that despite a decade of counselling, and all of my tools as an educator and a BodyTalk practitioner, I couldn't will or think myself out of.

The night prior, in a moment of frustration, I had raised my voice at my 6-year-old son when he refused to go back to his bed and go to sleep because he was too scared to be in his room by himself. Bedtime had slipped away from us that night and it was late. The little boys needed to go to sleep and I had so much work to do - like always. I had an intense headache. There was no time for extra stories, or any patience left to be a *soft and gentle* mom. I was counting down every minute until I could have a few minutes of silence and solitude on my own - until I could fully exhale and breathe in my own space.

The truth is, it wasn't really about the late bedtime, the refusal of my son to sleep in his own bed, or all the extra work I had left to do that night. My mental and emotional state was a domino effect of the residual emotions swirling from the stressful week, the pandemic lock-downs, as well as the huge backpack of grief and emotion I continued to carry from the past that had not yet been fully resolved. All of it erupted into anger again and everyone in my house was at the other end of it. Silently beating myself up inside, I knew I could do better, yet at that moment, my train had definitely derailed, again.

Good mothers would never yell. Good mothers stay calm and don't get angry. Good mothers would never make their children cry.

"*Be Good to Yourself.*" - words from my psychologist, Jeanette, often ring through my head on hard days. I anchor to that phrase when I stumble on this motherhood journey, often falling short according to my own expectations. Even as I write this, the ball and chain of mom guilt is sitting right here with me, like a heavy weight on my chest. I know what overwhelms me and what stresses contribute to that overwhelm. I sometimes fool myself into thinking that I've become a master of this balancing act - that I can, in fact, do it all with no problem, all of the time. I've learned the hard way, that I can't. Juggling the roles of mother, wife, and ex-wife also includes the role of a house cleaner, cook, birthday cake baker, chauffeur, party planner, accountant, and whatever else is required of me, weighs me down. I not only have to take a step back sometimes, but I also need to take a break. It's ok to take a break. It doesn't mean you love your family any less. It means you love yourself enough to know when it's time to put yourself at the top of your priority list.

Everything we see, read, and hear about motherhood is full of love and joy, cuddles and hugs, freshly baked buns, and nice tidy beds. Not a single expectation or conversation I had about motherhood prepared me for the realness of some of the darker moments like divorce, burn-out, addiction, death, loss, and immense grief. One particular night, after struggling with self-doubt, mom guilt, and wishing I were different in more ways than one as a mother, my husband, Alan, looked at me and said, "I don't see inadequacy, Laura. You see it, but I don't see it. I see a damn good mother. " Often the best and truest view we could ever get of ourselves is that through the eyes of those who love us most - our parents, our spouses, our children, or our own siblings.

I'm not sure I could ever really *see it*. From the time I was a young teen, I struggled to find my sense of self-worth. Reading through my teenage diary in preparation for this book I found myself overwhelmed with tears and the realization that thirty years later, my struggles look awfully familiar to those of my 15-year-old self.

Over the years I've acquired many new tools (and people) to add to my mental health maintenance plan that help me process the little and big traumas that led me where I am today. One of those new tools was putting pen to paper, and writing, which led me on this author journey. My path has not been straight and clear but rather has taken quite a few twists and turns. There were times when I felt like I had completely lost my way and lost who I was. I'm still not sure if I know who I *really* am. What I know to be true is that not all storms come into our lives to disrupt them, some come with a purpose to clear a fresh path and lead us into growth and discovery of new paths we did not know were awaiting us.

Strong as a Mother

The yin energy that gives life, guides, heals and upholds this planet is beautifully sacred. Historically, it's been the anchor of many tribes, cultures, and communities across the world for centuries - guiding and nurturing families through hardships, sorrow, and loss. What each of us on this planet has in common is that we all have a mother. Our lives begin on the inside of our mother's wombs, literally tethered to her by a single lifeline. We share the frequencies that run through her body and mind without conscious awareness. Our mother's body, an incredible vessel of nourishment, nurtures our mind, body, and spirit for approximately 280 days. The moment her eyes meet ours, we know innately, that she is *home.*

The crown of motherhood is both an incredible gift and one of the heaviest burdens a woman will ever carry. Her identity is forever changed the moment she discovers the potential for life that exists inside of her, yet it will take a lifetime to realize how much her identity is tied to this reality. From sacrifice to sorrow, grit and guilt, joy and judgement - she'll earn every badge along the journey. She's doubted herself a thousand times and then some more. With tools in her tool belt that she's been given from generations that mothered before her, she will do the best that she can, and yet there will be so many times when that won't feel like it's nearly good enough. She stoically and proudly wears the masks of strength and resilience, courage and willpower, yet underneath she may be anything but confident. Her worthiness is often dependent on how well she is able to serve and care for others, especially those she loves. She wears her motherhood suit of armour proudly, yet there will be chinks in her armour that she must work through.

The fairytale mother-child relationship may not fit the hand that some of us have been dealt. As daughters, we may seek to understand her, yet never fully get there. We may not even feel that coveted deep connection to her. Nonetheless, she is your mother. Perhaps, she is no longer in your life or never was. Perhaps another 'mother' stepped in and took her place, showing you that unconditional love is possible, and a bloodline isn't the only requirement for 'family'.

Earning the title of *mother* is expected if you are a woman, whether you feel it's the right path for you or not. There is judgement, expectation, societal norms and roles you'll be asked to fit neatly into. Not all of us will fit inside *the box*. I'm not sure any of us fit inside of the box at all, yet we sure strive to.

That woman is me. She is you. She is our neighbour, our sister, our friend, our daughter, and our grandmother. She has a voice, dreams, doubts, and a divine purpose. Her fears will often lead the way down her path but she'll rarely let you see them. A peak behind closed doors is not often one she will grant permission to see. There will be pain hidden and truths silenced, all for the greater good of those she loves.

The journey to and through motherhood is arduous and burdensome but is also full of beauty, wonder, and joy. It's a rollercoaster ride with the highest of highs and the lowest of lows, and we are never fully prepared for what it has to offer at the next stage. There is no guide or map, but rather mentors who offer a hand to hold along the way.

I became a mother later than I wanted to but sooner than I was actually ready. Seventeen years into the motherhood journey I am still learning and growing through my self-doubts, biggest fears, and honest mistakes every single day. I am proud and so blessed to have stepped into this beautiful mask of motherhood to four amazing souls.

Each of my children is unique in their own way - teaching and guiding me through some of the most important life lessons.

This book is inspired by my own journey of motherhood and that of other women in my circle, whose stories of strength, courage, perseverance and grit, moved me to begin something a few years ago that I called the *Strong as a Mother: Coffee & Conversation* series. For each edition, I invited a panel of mothers, sisters, grandmothers, and caregivers to share their journeys of womanhood, motherhood, marriage, mental health and everything in between. Hundreds of women came together to laugh, cry, grow and heal over coffee and conversation. The movement even survived the pandemic of 2020 as I took the platform online and welcomed more women from across the country, and beyond its borders, into the *Strong as a Mother* circle.

Through these pages, I offer you a look inside this movement as I share a collection of personal memoirs from a handful of some of the many inspirational women I have been fortunate to cross paths with. Each one has been put on my path in a synchronistic and purposeful way. They have each offered a unique perspective and lens of awareness into my own inner self - a mirror for my own healing. For that, I am forever grateful to each of them. May their stories offer an extra hand to hold along your way - a solid place for your heart to land as you connect with their hearts through their stories of strength and resilience. May you share in the collective joy and pain of their journeys.

Even though women are wired for connection, what we often lose is the important connection we have with ourselves. We can quickly become lost in the journey of nurturing and caring for others, putting the needs of our loved ones ahead of our own. Sometimes the way back to ourselves is paved with difficult lessons and immense growth. In our journey to experiencing full, joyful and deeply connected lives, there are times when we feel disconnected and alone. That's been the beauty of the *Strong as a Mother* movement - authentic and honest connection. What started as a wild and crazy idea to invite a few women to get together and chat over coffee turned into something that brought so much healing into my own life.

I promise you that what we all share is an unwavering desire to *get it right* with those we love. We all carry burdens of pain with us that influence the way we walk through this life and the way we connect with others. Each of us is on a unique path to resolve that pain and leave the least amount of collateral damage on our loved ones. We don't always get it right. We were never meant to get it right, but when we practice grace and gratitude, the wounds heal quicker and the mistakes feel lighter.

When my own personal journey of motherhood took an unexpected turn, I was tested and challenged in ways I had never imagined. Yet, had that unexpected turn never happened, I wouldn't be writing this book today. A peek behind my *closed door* and those of the brave and beautiful women in this book will offer you a soft place to land if you find yourself struggling with any aspect of motherhood, marriage or mental health. I've discovered that no one gets it right all of the time. In fact, many times we get it wrong the first time, but that's where the beauty of growth lies on this journey.

When the Light Goes Out

The quickest way to see the glowing spark from a 6-year-old's bright blue eyes fade is to tell her that her dad is moving out. In a fraction of a second, her entire life falls apart and there's not a damn thing you can do to put the pieces back. There will always and forever be *life before* and *life after* that moment.

We rehearsed it over and over and over again, my ex-husband and I, selecting just the *right* words we would use to make it as easy as we could on her. Were we trying to make it easy on her or easier on ourselves to lessen the immense burden of guilt we both were carrying? The truth is, there is no easy way to break that kind of news to a child of any age. It is painful and heartbreaking, and it will continue to be for a very long time.

It was incredibly heart-wrenching, the whole ordeal. Certainly not the fairy tale ending I had dreamed our family of four would have. It's a day that's forever etched in my memory. Looking back it honestly felt like leading a tiny tender lamb to slaughter when we called her to come upstairs from her room and sit with us at the kitchen island to break the news to her. I felt sick to my stomach. I remember vividly her soft dirty blonde curls and the look on her face when she saw us both and immediately sensed that something bad was about to happen.

"Honey, we both love you very, very much…."

The time between "Honey, we love you." and "Your dad is going to move out for a bit." is all a blur. I don't even remember which one of us actually spoke the words, but I think I made him do it. Yes, I made him do it. He *chose* this and so he should shoulder most of the guilt. He broke my heart, and I knew that if I made him break hers, he might feel as much pain as I had. At least that's how I felt at that moment. The truth was both of our hearts were broken. Damage was done that couldn't be undone. Those early days washed so much sadness over all of us. We were all in pain and each of us felt it and processed it in very different ways.

Once we broke the news, she buried her delicate sandy blond curls in her hands, with her head resting on the kitchen island and wept. She was sobbing. He was sobbing. I was sobbing. It is indeed one of the saddest moments of my life.

I had always thought that if there was a *good way* to break the news to your kids that you were separating, we had found it. I believed that we had chosen the best words possible to spare her at least a little bit of pain. Since that tear-filled, confusing, and painful day, she and I had never really spoken about it again.

It was like the elephant in the room. I never asked how she felt about the day we told her that life-changing news and she never shared - until the day she did. It turns out that our carefully selected plan of telling her was the worst way we could've broken the news to her. It's not *what* we said that really crushed her - but rather, what we didn't say.

These days, as my teenage daughter steps bravely into navigating her own residual pain from being a child of a divorced home, there are days when she is comfortable opening up to me about having her entire world come crashing down on her at six years old. Those fleeting conversations usually happen while we are driving in a car together. *Life tip* - save the hard discussions with your teen until you're driving in the car together because, well, because they can't leave.

We were driving into the city one day when she and I started talking about a family we knew with small children who were starting to navigate a divorce. I asked for her opinion, as a kid, regarding the best way to break that kind of news to your children, so I could share that insight with the parents.

I said, "Hey, a friend of mine is really upset and wants some advice about how she should tell her daughters that she and her husband would be separating. I told her I would ask you because I've never been a kid who's experienced that, but you have."

She looked over at me with a fierceness in her eyes and said, "Well, tell her not to lie to them about it."

"Pardon me, sweetheart? What do you mean lie?", even though I already knew where she was going with this.

"Well mom, you and dad lied to me."

I took a big breath, paused, and said, "We actually didn't lie."

My daughter replied, "Yes. You. Did. You told me that you and dad needed to take some time to figure things out so he would be moving out of our house. You never said he wouldn't ever be coming back."

Instantly a lump formed in my throat and tears began to well up in my eyes. She wasn't wrong and I had no words for her. We never said he'd be coming back because we both knew he wasn't. We knew if we told her that he wasn't coming back, it would break her little heart even more. *Life tip* - there's no way to sugarcoat pain.

Our son was only two years old at the time so we couldn't really explain to him what was happening. He did ask where his daddy was and would often cry for him at bedtime. He spent many nights sleeping with me in my bed and sensing my sadness, would comfort me with his hugs, snuggles and "I love you's" as much as he could. I remember one day he saw me speaking on the phone to my sister and I was crying uncontrollably. He came over and begged me to put the phone down as it was making me sad. I won't forget that moment and the sincerity in his voice and the look of empathy in his eyes.

A decade later all of us: my daughter, my son, my ex-husband, and I are still carrying pieces of the residual pain from the divorce with us and still trying to unpack all of the emotions, memories, and challenges that come with it. For my two older children and me, there will always be life before the divorce and life after the divorce. Life after the divorce has brought me a kind of love and personal growth that I didn't know was possible. It brought me a kind of love and connection on a soul level that I didn't know existed. It has also given my two oldest children a loving and caring step-father and two little brothers to grow through life with. We don't always get it right. In fact, we put the *fun* in dysfunction and there's often more chaos than calm, but we love each other fiercely and share a solid loyalty as a blended family.

There are often times I wonder how things are going to turn out for my two older children, having come from a divorced home during their formative years. I can only understand the entire experience through my lens and do my best to try to understand it from their perspective. I tried so hard throughout the early months and years of that divorce to shelter them from the ripple-effect pain that rocked their little worlds. In a small town, nothing really stays private and our divorce had a few extra *juicy layers* that most certainly got the attention of the public.

None of the storybooks we read to our children ever paint pictures of the darker moments that families might experience together. When we start our own journeys of motherhood we rarely think or talk about the chapters of struggle - infertility, divorce, illness, addiction, or death. Those are chapters we get to live out and navigate on our own. The darker moments of motherhood are rarely talked openly and freely about: the miscarriages, the sleepless nights, the overwhelm, the mental exhaustion, the doubt, the guilt, or the grief that we will experience as mothers. We just never know when that grief is about to knock on our door.

Over the last decade, I've met so many women who have sat in those darker moments; holding on to love, faith, prayer, and hope. I've been incredibly inspired by their stories of courage, strength, and resilience. What each and every one of them has in common, is grit and steadfast conviction to bring themselves, and their families out the other side of the darkness and back into the light. They do it with grace, humbleness, and deep wisdom of what is best for them and their loved ones.

In times of deep pain and uncertainty in my life, it's been the yin energy that surrounded me - the connections I had with my sister, mother, grandmother, aunts, and female friends, that helped lift me back up again. That's a unique gift that we have to offer one another and a gift I hope you find in the stories that are shared in this book.

Bring Charlie Home

It was five years ago that I was laying in my bed one November night, a week after we had been home from taking a family trip to Disney World, scrolling through Facebook when a GoFundMe fundraising request popped up in my newsfeed. The title was *"Bring Charlie Home"* and as soon as I saw it, I felt a twinge in my stomach and this strong pull to click on the link and read it. I read the story, I wept, and I immediately donated money to help bring Charlie home. Even though I didn't have a clue who Charlie was, my heart felt a calling to help this mother and her family.

The story about Charlie and his family stayed with me for quite some time, tugging at my heartstrings. My husband even commented that it seemed to really be consuming my mind and thoughts. About a year later, I had a new BodyTalk client was referred to me for a session. At the time, I didn't know her, and she didn't know me. Often, in a BodyTalk session, there will be a priority of releasing stored emotion from a certain organ, endocrine gland, or body part. In this session, I almost immediately had a keen and very strong awareness of grief settled in the lungs of this woman as she lay down on my table. I looked at her and said, "I have a strong awareness of the emotion of grief that's being held in the lungs." She turned her head and looked at me with deep sadness in her eyes and said, "That would make sense. It's almost the one-year anniversary of the death of my nephew." It was at that immediate moment that I knew her nephew was Charlie. I don't know how I knew - but I just knew. I looked at her and said, "This is going to sound incredibly crazy but, is your nephew's name Charlie?" It was almost as if time had stood still for a moment and then she looked at me, her eyes wide with disbelief, with a quiet voice and said, "Yes - how did you know?" I don't know how I knew, but I do know that there may have been a divine intervention at work to bring us together.

Charlie's aunt Heather and I became good friends and a few years later, she recommended that I reach out to Charlie's mom, Camille, and invite her to be a guest on the *Strong as a Mother Coffee & Conversation* series to share her journey of grief and healing as a mother. I was very apprehensive as I felt this was such a very tender and tragic story, but Heather reassured me that Camille would welcome the invite. I did indeed reach out to Camille and she appeared as a guest on one of the Mother's Day virtual editions during the pandemic. It was a heart-wrenching edition, the celebration of life, love and the story of a little boy who left a huge imprint on the hearts of those who loved him. What I didn't know before I invited Camille to share her story was that she had suffered more trauma in her life than I could've ever even imagined and still, she continued to put one foot in front of the other to do the best she could for the people she loved - the epitome of a strong mother.

Shaken Faith

CAMILLE BARZEELE

I was born the oldest of five children with my youngest brother and I being thirteen years apart. I was a very quiet, shy girl who loved to spend time reading. We went to Church multiple times a week as we were raised in a very strict, serious Christian home. We were well-loved and it was a happy childhood.

Our religion, being an offshoot of the Quakers, meant we wore only dresses - no make-up or jewelry. School was hard and we were all bullied quite badly because we were so different. We had no TV, we dressed differently - we just stood out and I remember hating it. We weren't allowed to hang out with the kids in school as we mostly stayed close to the people in our Church, but with a family as big as ours, we always had a buddy. Following my Gr. 12 graduation, my parents decided to leave that religion which tore everything away that we ever knew, including our social circle. I lost all of my friends and my whole social life revolved around the Church. It felt like starting over and I was 19. My parents had been a part of that Church for over forty years and so it was even more difficult for them.

I moved to go to university and met my husband, Clark when I was 20 years old. We fell in love and got married three years later. Neither of us finished our degree as we decided to go into business with his uncle in Tim Horton's franchises, which we've been a part of for fifteen years now. I so appreciate the lifestyle it affords me as I can be there for my children when they need me, but it does come with its' own unique challenges.

Growing up, I always knew that I wanted to be a mother. When my mother was pregnant with my youngest brother, I wanted that baby so badly! We had a very close relationship, and to this day, he's one of my closest siblings. Clark and I knew we wanted kids together and my ultimate goal was always six children.

Clark and I got married and then found out were pregnant with our firstborn, Liam, about a month after. He was our first little miracle baby. The pregnancy was difficult and I was so sick that I was hospitalized three times. I was so dehydrated because I couldn't keep anything down. I was in labour for five days with him. You don't know what you don't know when it's your first pregnancy, so I was just going along thinking, "Well, this must be what labour is like."

When they finally called in an obstetrician because his heart rate was dropping they discovered it was his shoulder that was stuck, not his head - they had been vacuuming on his shoulder to try and get him out. It felt like a dream - the dark room, with doctors and nurses around. They had the whole NICU team and the obstetric team there. One nurse was pushing him out by putting pressure on my stomach, another doctor was on the vacuum and a second one was on the forceps and they literally just yanked as hard as they could to get him out. His APCAR score was 2 when he was first born but he bounced back quickly - he's literally a miracle child. We had to take him to physio for a year for his neck and his shoulder as he was injured from the labour and delivery. That was the start of my motherhood journey.

I got pregnant about a year later and at our 20-week scan they realized the baby had a genetic fatal condition called Meckel-Gruber, a trisomy issue that results in an unviable pregnancy, and I delivered our second baby at 23 weeks gestation. The hardest part was going to the hospital knowing that we wouldn't be bringing a baby home. The one thing that did offer a little comfort to us is that we did get to hold her and name her - we named her Ceri. Seeing how incredibly sick she was, and holding her tiny body, knowing that she never could've survived, was such an emotional experience. It was the deepest grief I had felt in life to that point. My husband bought me a ring with two bands and a pearl, as that was her birthstone, just to remember her and I still wear that ring in memory of my sweet Ceri.

We were told by the doctors that this genetic condition Ceri had would affect 1 in 4 babies. We did all of the genetic testing and found out that we were both recessive carriers of the gene, but I definitely wanted more kids, so we got pregnant quite quickly again. The doctors did scans on me much earlier this time and at 17 weeks we discovered that we had another little boy with the same genetic condition. I delivered him at 20 weeks and we named him Declan. We went through the same heartbreak as before, with disbelief as they'd said "1 in 4", so we had such strong hope. It was devastating, so heart-crushing. It definitely shook my faith, and I wondered often what I had done wrong in life to deserve this kind of grief as a mother.

All I wanted to be was a mom, and so we clung on to hope that this wasn't the end for us and that our family would continue to grow. We looked into adoption after losing Declan as it had always been on my heart but had gotten pregnant a third time with the hope that we would be able to have a healthy baby. Yet again, we were told this baby had the same fatal condition. We delivered our baby girl, Amani, at 20 weeks gestation with more heartache. It just didn't seem possible that this could happen to us three pregnancies in a row.

We were so hopeful for a bigger family, so we looked into InVitro fertilization with implantation genetics and started that process. We did one round and we were able to get 18 embryos, but only 2 of those embryos were viable with life.

On Clark's birthday, May 3rd, 2012 we got a call from Social Services that we had been matched for adoption with a little boy and little girl - William, age 5, and Joy, age 6. They were full siblings and by June 14th they had moved into our home. They had been in nine different foster homes prior to coming to us. It was like getting two infants even though they were much older. They were up in the middle of the night and they couldn't communicate their needs. William was so delayed that he still couldn't walk or talk at the age of 5, so he just screamed as his way of communication. We had to carry him places because he couldn't walk. We were so grateful to get these two wonderful children and have them as part of our family, but I was so exhausted.

After Joy and William moved in with us we did our first round of InVitro and it ended in a miscarriage. I was preparing for the second round of implantation and as part of that process, they have you take a pregnancy test to ensure that you're not pregnant so that they could go ahead with the drugs they need to give you. Miraculously and shockingly, I was pregnant. I was so stunned to get that result - it was literally a miracle. I was very anxious as my last 3 natural pregnancies had resulted in this incredible heartache and loss so I was very nervous. We got to the 15-week scan and found out that we were having a healthy baby - no fatal genetic condition this time. I was able to carry this baby to 40 weeks and delivered a very healthy, 9-pound baby boy, Charlie Felix, on January 7th, 2014.

This beautiful boy was wanted so badly by all of us. Joy had said from the time she had moved in with us that she was praying every day that she could have a baby sister or brother. He was so well-loved and because of that, he never got put down. He was confident and outgoing, and also very chatty! Charlie was a firecracker and a ray of sunshine all in one. At just two and a half years old he could talk clearly. It was the happiest years of our lives as he was just such a ray of sunshine with his white-blond hair - he looked like sunshine! He would watch out the window for the big kids to come home from school and yell out, "Here come my friends! Here come my friends!" Charlie made our family complete. He was the piece of the puzzle that was missing and our family felt whole with him. Just as everything felt like it was finally falling into place with our family, our lives took a turn in a devastating direction.

We took an annual family vacation every fall to DisneyWorld In Florida as it's the most magical place on earth. That fall we rented a house with a pool in the backyard and my parents came along with us. The morning of November 11th, we were getting ready to go to the park, the kids were eating breakfast and I was making lunches when I turned around and asked if anyone had seen Charlie as I couldn't see or hear him. We all started looking for him. I went into the backyard, looked in the pool, and found Charlie in it wearing his swimming gear as we were going to a water park later that day. He had always loved the water so much. We immediately called the paramedics as he was unresponsive and he was rushed to the local Children's Hospital. The doctors told us they believed he had been in the water for less than two minutes.

It was the darkest part of my life. I can't imagine what I would've done without my parents there with us. When we called the rest of our family back home in Canada to tell them there had been an accident, every single one of them got on a plane and flew down to be with us. We were surrounded by the love of family at the darkest time of our lives.

They had two rooms for us at the hospital, one for Charlie and one for the family right beside him. On the morning of November 12th, we knew that it was just a matter of time before we had to say goodbye to him. Clark called a family meeting with all of us and he said, "This was an accident. There is nobody to blame. We will continue to be a family and we will not lay blame on anyone." And we never have - no one ever blamed each other for what had happened.

We were able to spend the whole day with Charlie and I was able to hold him for what felt like 5 minutes to me, but my sister said it was 5 hours. I was holding him as they called all of our family into the room and all of the sudden I felt his little body lift out of my arms. Although I was still holding him, and his body was there, I felt a weight being lifted away, out of my arms - I knew he was gone. I felt it, he was gone. I felt my baby boy being lifted to heaven.

By the grace of God, we had those we loved there with us. I don't know how we would've gotten through any of it without them. My in-laws took the next flight home and took our kids with them so we were able to stay a bit longer to make the preparations for Charlie to come home. In those darkest days, I remember begging my mother to give me more pills that the doctor had prescribed for me to sleep because I just couldn't handle the pain. I can't even describe the pain. My heart literally felt like it was going to explode and I wanted to die. There was more than one time I didn't think I could survive the immense, crushing grief.

But I had these three other little faces looking to me for comfort and love. They needed me and they were missing their brother too - so much. It took every ounce of my being to wake up in the morning and get out of bed. Often, I would just get up, feed the kids, get them off to school and then go back to bed until 3:30 pm when they got back home.

We had family stay with us for a few weeks after the accident. One of my very best friends was dedicated to supporting me and after a few months, she would come and make me go for a walk every single day. She'd come into my bedroom, get me out of bed, and make me go walking with her. That saved my life - to just get out of bed and go for a walk. I truly believe it saved my life. I had to start putting the pieces back together again.

Clark and I started to see a grief counsellor together and joined Compassionate Friends of Saskatoon, a grief support group of parents who have lost children. We reached out to all the support we could. We couldn't wrap our minds around the fact that we prayed for this baby for so long and then he was taken from us in the blink of an eye. We needed all the light we could get in a very dark space in our life.

Once again, our faith was shaken when we lost Charlie, but in a way, it was also cemented. It was hard to believe that God was even real. How could he do this to us? After everything we had been through? Ironically enough, it was the church who really supported us, by sending meals and coming to see us as we began to process the grief. We even joined a bible study group. During the first six months, anyone who stopped by our home was very much welcome to bring light in.

Throughout the grief process after the loss of Charlie, there was never a point where our marriage was shaken. We had been told that most marriages wouldn't survive this kind of grief. We learned early through counselling that Clark and I grieve very differently, and we could not judge each other because of it. When I was having a down day, Clark would pick me up and vice versa. I remember laying on the floor one day in our bedroom just bawling my head off and I just couldn't stop. I told Clark that I didn't think I could continue to live like this forever and he said to me, "It's ok Camille. We are going to just do everything together. I'll be there with you. It's going to be ok." So that's what we did for a long time - we did everything together.

Kids grieve so differently than adults. Our kids would go to school and reports from the school and their teachers would be that they were doing very well - they were happy, doing well with their friends, but they would come home and be little miseries with us. They still cry for Charlie. Our daughter still sleeps in our room. Liam shared a room with Charlie since he was born and it was devastating for him to lose his little buddy. We still lay with Liam to go to sleep at night. There will never be a day that goes by that we don't miss and think of our Charlie.

Part of our healing journey with Charlie is to honour his memory every year with a golf tournament held at Dakota Dunes. We raise money for the Tim Horton's Kids Camps to send underprivileged youth to camps who wouldn't otherwise have the opportunity to go. Charlie had everything he ever wanted. He was a happy, outgoing, confident little boy and that's what we want for other children too. We want them to feel confident and we want them to have fun at camp! We have raised almost half a million dollars so far and have been able to send many, many kids to camp all over Canada. The amount of support we've received has been unbelievable - it's really taken on a life of its own.

Each year, on November 11th and 12th, we have a memorial service graveside for Charlie. We all gather as a family and share memories of him. A good friend of ours usually writes a poem. Also, on June 14th, we remember our adoption day and I always put up a "Family is Forever" sign with Charlie in it too because we celebrate that we are and always will be a family together.

I still have pain and flashbacks of the accident and there are definitely days that I struggle. I don't cry myself to sleep every night anymore, and I'm able to laugh again, not as much as I used to, but I'm able to find laughter and joy again.

For any mothers reading my story who are navigating the pain of child loss or any type of grief, I want to offer you hope - you will get through it. The pain will never go away, but eventually, it isn't as searing as it was in the beginning. It's like navigating a storm. At first, you're trying to wade through water that's at your neck, and you can barely move. You feel as if you're going to drown at any moment. Eventually, the water level drops to your waist, and you can begin to take steps just a little bit easier. As time continues on, the water level falls to your knees, and you can walk a little bit easier and eventually it's just a puddle at your feet and you can get through it.

I probably hug and kiss my kids these days more than they appreciate it, but I just can't help myself. I still worry more than normal that I might lose one of them and that any moment could be my very last moment with them. Truthfully, I hope that my children will want to live at home forever - that would be just fine for me! I want to be involved in their life and be the kind of Grandma who helps out with her grandchildren. My wish for my family is that they are happy and fulfilled. I want them to know that they are so loved - always.

One Day at a Time

The journey back from the depths of grief is a different road for every person who walks it, but it always begins by taking it one day at a time. I remember sitting with Camille, face to face during our interview, choking back my own tears, and thinking about the searing pain her heart withstood through all of the loss she experienced. How could her heart still be beating after that immense amount of crushing grief it had to withstand? I also noticed though how her eyes lit up with joy when she spoke about Charlie and the smile that warmed her face when she said his name. The love she had for her sweet boy was just as big as her grief, and it was her love for him and her other children that kept her going.

I've spoken to so many women who've navigated the path of grief, the absolute darkest path being the loss of a child, and every one of them has said that they kept going because they simply had to; there was no other choice, other than death itself. The depth of grief from the loss of a child is so painful and indescribable that there are no words that can even compare to the immense crushing heartbreak that a mother is left with when she outlives her own child. Although I have not experienced it, like any woman reading this book, it has always been one of my greatest fears since becoming a mother.

Grief can knock on our door for so many different reasons throughout the journey of motherhood; death, illness, divorce, moving your family, the loss of a job, having a special needs child, having your child experience adversity, parenting during a pandemic, and even just seeing our children grow up through the different stages of childhood can bring with it grief. Any change in a familiar pattern in our lives results in grieving a loss, whether it be a small wave of grief or a tsunami that wipes our feet out from underneath us.

Our minds harness so much more power than most of us will ever realize. You never know what *strong* is until you're put in a situation that gives you no other choice than to be strong. No matter what adversity or challenge we face in life, the journey through it always starts by taking it one day at a time.

I come from a long line of strong women who've experienced their share of grief in life. My Oma, the rock and foundation of my mom's family, and undoubtedly one of the most inspirational women in my life, shared with me a poem that kept her going through some of her darkest days. I had it painted on a wall hanging that is in our home. It's called 'One Day at a Time' and I read it every single, day as I walk down the stairs to start my day.

Help me believe what I could be, all that I am. Show me the stairway I have to climb. Lord, for my sake, teach me to take, one day at a time.

Oma had solid roots in her faith and growing up, and learning her story, I now understand why. She was just a young girl, not yet a teenager, living in Czechoslovakia during WWII, when her father, a peacekeeper, was shot at by Croatian freedom fighters and killed. Living in Czechoslovakia as a German, during a time of ethnic cleansing, meant she couldn't go to school. The Germans also had a curfew and couldn't go out after dark. She was made to wear an armband so that she stood out as a German.

When she was 13, her mother, sister, and grandmother were forced from their home. They were warned by a neighbour who had interned at a communist labour camp, that they'd be "heading West". They were permitted to take 20 kilos each of personal belongings and buried some of their most treasured items in their backyard - in case they were able to return. As they were driven away on the back of wagons, they could see the soldiers raiding their home. My Oma, her mother, sister, and grandmother were taken to a refugee camp in southern Germany from September 1946 to the spring of 1947. Her mother, refusing to keep her family there because there was Typhoid in the camp, left the camp and moved her girls to a small town in Bavaria. She was a lace maker since she was 9 years old and then learned how to sew and knit. They would trade their hand-knit socks for food and goods - the whole town practically was wearing their socks!

On October 7, 1955, with only twenty dollars in her pocket, Oma came to Canada on the Rosa Star ship. The ship landed in Halifax and she then took a train to Humboldt, Saskatchewan. She married a German man, my Opa, whom she had met while she was still in Germany and came to Canada the year prior; sponsored to work as a mechanic. They had a family of five with one son and four daughters.

Oma rarely talked about growing up during the War or any of the other burdens she carried in life. Not only did she have to grieve leaving her home behind again when she moved to Canada, but she also left her sister and mother with the great divide of the Atlantic Ocean between them. Later on in her life, she went through a divorce and had to bury a daughter, my aunt Barbara, who died at the age of 47 after a courageous 7-year battle with ovarian cancer. She was one strong woman but Oma carried the most painful pieces of her story with her in her body. Her lungs and heart were both heavy and clouded with grief, and she developed COPD and congestive heart failure.

The day she died our family tree was shaken and the strongest of the roots had been unearthed. The rest of the tree, now unsteady without its' main root, was left to find a way to keep growing without its' main anchor. She was the lighthouse we all turned to when we were lost. She was the glue that kept us all together. Her laughter, soft gentle eyes, familiar scents and thick German accent, just felt like home. She had a fierce and strong spirit, but her hands and home were always open to welcome those she loved.

When she took her last breath it was my sister, Anna-Marie, who was the nurse by her side. It was my sister who saw her rapid decline and knew the dreaded end we had all feared had finally come. It was my sister who had to hold space for my mother and my aunts as they said their unexpected last goodbyes to the woman whom we had all secretly hoped would live forever. It was my sister who had to help prepare Oma to send her to the funeral home. I don't know how she harnessed the strength to be the anchor that day for Oma as she transitioned from this world to the next, but I know that the good Lord works in mysterious ways and that having her there with Oma as she finally was released of all of her pain, was by divine design.

My sister is the best nurse I'll ever know. She's brilliant with her knowledge of nursing and her attention to detail is second to none. She gives selflessly as a nurse and is dedicated to giving nothing but the best care to those she tends to. She's a critical and quick thinker, asks questions many won't, and pushes when others don't, just to ensure that her patients get the best care. She is exactly the kind of nurse you want by your side to advocate for you in a time of need. She's a rare commodity in the world of health professionals, and I'm so damn proud to call her my sister.

Her life too has been steeped in grief, and although she's always been my little sister, she's carried with her wisdom and strength well beyond her years. She was my anchor and carried me through my dark, empty days of sadness during the early months of my marriage breakdown. She would sit on the other end of the phone and hold space for me for hours on end, at any time of day, always reminding me of my own worth and value as a wife, woman, and mother.

I never knew the depths of some of her pain and grief until I sat down with her to do the interview for this book. As I listened to her share her story of motherhood with me, there were times when I felt sad and shameful for not knowing some of her story, but more so, not being there for her during those times. It felt almost like I was interviewing a stranger - such an odd feeling. I asked her why she never had said any of this to me before and she responded, "We just didn't talk about those things in our family." It wasn't until she said that, that I realized, although our family was closer than many, there were still things that we just didn't talk about. Here we were, many years later, two sisters, having a heart-to-heart about motherhood.

Whatever it Takes

ANNA-MARIE BAUMANN

I always loved kids so I had no doubt that I would be a mother but one of the first things I discovered as a mother was that kids are so much easier to care for when they're not our own. I thought motherhood would be joyous, but for me, more than often, it was not. I thought it would be easy, but soon realized it was anything but. Miscarriages, premature births, NICU stays, screaming babies, physical and mental health challenges, and learning disabilities. I didn't imagine facing the obstacles I did as a mother or the difficulties that my kids would face growing up in a world that's not so accommodating to kids who are *outside of the box.* Motherhood was full of unexpected challenges; including conception, my ability to sustain life, and delivery. They say that pregnancy is supposed to be a time of joy, connection, and celebration, but for me, it was never-ending chaos. I was always waiting for the other shoe to drop. I was taken off work quite early in both pregnancies due to complications. This left me feeling a bit disconnected as I spent most of both pregnancies expecting the worst each time a new or reoccurring issue arouse. Also, with each pregnancy came the loss of a grandparent. Both my husband's grandmother and my Opa were the first family members to learn about our pregnancies - we whispered the news in their ear the day each passed away.

I never thought I would meet our first son, Lucas. After 17 weeks of spotting, months of bed rest, severe nausea, and high blood pressure, he entered the world three weeks early via C-section. In his first two days of life, Lucas was pretty mellow but after that, he screamed and cried, day and night, for three months straight. My husband was away at work and so I was parenting on my own for stretches of time. Fearing being seen as a failure at motherhood, I didn't want to ask other family members for help. I tried anything and everything I could and would take him back to the doctor over and over again. They just kept patting me on the back and saying, "You're just a tired, new mom."

At the three-month mark, I couldn't take it anymore and when I took him to see the doctor that time, I firmly stated that I wasn't going back home until they figured out what was wrong. Within 15 minutes of being seen, and one urine sample, we found out that he had a bladder infection. After three days of antibiotics, he quit crying. From that moment on he was a really good baby. I held onto the guilt of him suffering unnecessarily those first three months and was angry that we were robbed of that bonding time because my concerns were not taken seriously. I always said that after making it through that any future pregnancy or infants should be a breeze. I later found out that one should never tempt the universe with such thoughts.

When we decided we were ready for another baby, my doctor suggested I take the same ovulation-stimulating medication we previously used and we got pregnant the first round. Alone at the first ultrasound, I found out that there were three babies, not just one. I was a little stunned and slightly panicked wondering all the way home how the hell we would ever manage this. We didn't share the pregnancy with anyone for another two months as my sister, had just had a miscarriage and I felt making our multiple pregnancy public at that time would be hurtful and cruel to her.

Around the 8-week mark, I experienced extensive hemorrhaging and we drove to emergency assuming that I was miscarrying. I was kept in a back room for hours with little contact, no medications, and no explanation. After five hours, they sent me home and told me to come back in a few days for an ultrasound. They said, "what will be, will be." We assumed that I had lost all three babies. The waiting was the worst part. At the ultrasound a few days later, I was told there were only two heartbeats, so I had lost one baby. During this ultrasound, they also discovered that I had partial placenta previa which further complicated matters. Again, I was off work for months before they were born and monitored closely.

I really struggled with how I felt after the miscarriage. At times I felt guilty that I had feelings of relief because I had no idea how we would manage three babies at once. Other times I was sad and wondered if that third baby was a boy or girl and what he/she would have looked like. I often dealt with those emotions by joking that the boys didn't want a girl in their club so they kicked her out, but I truly never dealt with the loss.

At 30 weeks, I saw a high-risk OBGYN who was concerned about the size difference between the boys. Jacob was always in the 3rd percentile while Wyatt was in the 90th. The chance of premature delivery was high. The doctor wanted to ensure that the boys had the best chance of survival, so she gave me the first of two steroid injections to support their lung development. When I came back a week later for the second injection I was informed, "You can't go home, you will be delivering these babies tomorrow." The specialist was worried the placental blood flow to Jacob was deteriorating and told me that if we didn't deliver as soon as possible, he could die.

The day our sons were born felt nothing like what I had imagined the day would be. I planned on natural births. I even started a hypnobirthing program, but the boys were born the next morning by C-Section at 31 weeks gestation. My husband and I knew they both would have to go to NICU. I was familiar with the process since I had started my nursing career in the neonatal intensive care unit (NICU). There were at least a dozen staff in the room during the delivery and the boys were whisked away to their stations as soon as they were born. Once stable enough for transfer, they were placed in incubators and taken to the NICU. I caught a quick glance as they were wheeled out of the room, but everything was a blur.

Upon entering the NICU with Dallas to meet our boys we were both hit with intense emotions. I was familiar with premature babies and all the tubes and sounds, but it is so different when they are your own babies on the other end of those tubes. Looking at their little, fragile bodies in such a vulnerable state was heartbreaking. With nothing else to do but take in every detail of their being, we took turns between both of them, tears running down our cheeks. The following day we went down to the gift shop and bought them two little stuffed animals - a giraffe for Wyatt as he was always the bigger one at 3 lbs 8 oz and a Lion for Jacob as he was and would continue to be a fighter, at 2 lbs 11 oz. These remained with them until they were discharged home.

NICU is a scary place to be in as you are surrounded by the sickest of babies. There were several sets of twins, and a few of them didn't make it during our stay there, and it's heart-wrenching. Having worked in NICU as a nurse I was used to holding extremely small babies and moving them with their cords and tubes. I knew the medications, understood the charts and monitor alarms, so that made our stay a lot less scary.

The boys were in NICU for 67 and 74 days and every single morning I was at rounds, filling two journals with details of each day: the doctor's orders, their weights, and what changed since the last report. Documenting was the only thing I had control of and how I passed my time while waiting hours at a time at their bedside. Children were not allowed in the NICU and I felt guilty each day I dropped our oldest son, Lucas, off at daycare or with family. I don't think he really understood what was going on or that he had brothers until the day they were both home. Financially it was a very difficult time for our family, being off work for so long, travelling back and forth daily, daycare, gas, groceries, monthly bills and specialty formula at the cost of $1500 a month resulted in a substantial amount of credit card debt.

The first six months at home were a chaotic blur. I consider us extremely lucky to have family and friends who were able to help us 24/7. Without them, we wouldn't have made it through as postpartum anxiety kicked in shortly after the boys came home. For the next four years we would travel back and forth to appointments for both boys. As preemies, they were automatically referred to the Kinsmen Children's Centre (KCC) and followed regularly by the neonatologist. The boys accessed speech, occupational, and physiotherapists during those appointments, utilizing different strategies and aids to assist in their development. Both boys met their milestones late and at different times which was stressful at times.

After several assessments, diagnostics, and a year-long wait list, Jacob received an autism spectrum disorder diagnosis (ASD) around 3 years of age and Wyatt was diagnosed with ADHD and anxiety a year later. When your child receives a diagnosis, it impacts you in ways you could never imagine. The fear of the unknown leads to grieving the life you thought your child would have and constant worry about what they will now have to endure. The reactions from friends and family vary and were sometimes met with denial or assumption of low IQ or inability to function.

Due to his ASD diagnosis, Jacob received more intensive therapies. Due to his sensitivities and aversions to eating food, we enrolled Jacob in an eight-week group that targeted sensory aversions to food. The children were taken into a room where there was a glass wall that the parents sat behind to observe the group. It broke my heart to sit there week after week watching as Jacob hid under the table with his face buried in the linoleum until the group was over. I left several sessions in tears fearful of what he was going to have to endure in life as he grows up. At the sixth session, he finally sat at the table but stared at the floor the entire time. and during the final two classes he progressed to touching some of the food. This transition brought such relief and although this didn't impact the variety, he was willing to eat at that time. This was the beginning of many more challenges to overcome.

We spent over a year on the waitlist for an assessment by a publicly funded pediatric psychiatrist for Wyatt. Lucas was struggling in school at that time and I was unable to get any assessments or assistance through the school so he was also referred to child psychiatry for assessment. Both boys were diagnosed with ADHD which was a tad confusing as they had completely opposite behaviours, but both excelled with stimulant medication.

Access to early intervention, therapists, and treatment was a breeze prior to entering school. However, once my kids entered kindergarten, there were next to no resources or supports I could access on a regular basis. The public school system was a nightmare for my kids and continues to be challenging. There is an enormous lack of understanding and resources related to mental, emotional, and cognitive health. Lucas struggled from kindergarten on and every time I would voice concerns and request assessments I would be met with the words "He is a boy and boys mature later." He was falling behind, constantly getting in trouble, and begging to stay home. It wasn't until he was diagnosed and treated for his ADHD that school got easier for him. He suddenly excelled at reading and was able to put more content into his assignments, yet he struggled to sit still and be quiet and got negative feedback for that.

When the twins were eligible to start play school, an ASD diagnosis meant Jacob was eligible for extra support. It has been found that intensive early intervention results in more successful outcomes for kids on the spectrum. I had to strongly advocate, provide letters from specialists/therapists, and be persistent to ensure that Jacob had the support of an educational assistant (EA) for the first two years. Because of the intensive early intervention and therapies, Jacob never stood out visually from the other kids, but this led to him getting lost in and misunderstood by the education system. It takes one-on-one instruction and review each time something new is taught to determine his level of understanding so that he can be given the appropriate strategies to help him succeed independently. After play school, individual EA support was rare.

When I think about my children's experience navigating school with their diagnosis and challenges, it makes me emotional. When you get told your kids are lazy and that "they could do it if they wanted to", it gets exhausting. Hearing comments like "You just need to try harder. If only you would apply yourself. Can't you just sit still?" really wears on a child after a while. The comments and judgement never seem to end. I felt like pounding my head against the wall more times than not throughout my boys' school years because of these struggles.

Over the years, to help the teachers understand my kids, I would sit down and put together an "All About Me" document, sharing with them what works well, and what doesn't for the boys. I would scan it and email it to their teachers. This way, they could know what to expect, what the kids like, what they're really good at, what they need some help with, and what doesn't work for them. I can't help but think if these educators would just take the time to really *know* my kids, their history, and background, perhaps they'd think twice before saying some of the things they've said to my boys. This is where I might ruffle some feathers, but if you're a teacher, please don't ever tell a child that they are lazy, or they need to just try harder, or sit still and they'd do better in school. Please just don't ever put anything negative in a report card for any child. Words matter and it really does affect their mental health.

At a very young age, we talked to the boys about everyone's uniqueness and how each of us sees and understands things differently from one another. That it is the same with others we meet throughout our lives. Our differences do not make us any less of a person. We did this intentionally as we knew the challenges they would face in a world that didn't always take kindly to people who were *outside of the box.*

One day Lucas came home and said, *"Mom, did you know that I have a disease? the teacher told me I have ADHD."* I never said aloud to my kids the name of their diagnosis. We never used labels, partly because I feared they would use them as a crutch or excuse instead of challenging themselves.

At the age of 9, my oldest son was diagnosed with major depressive disorder and suicidal ideation. We could see that his personality was changing but each time we reached out to the school we were told there were no concerns, and everything was fine in the classroom. When we talked to him, he didn't tell us what was going on. He didn't want to lose what little friends he had, even if they didn't treat him nicely. We had to move him to another school as a result of bullying and the effect it had on his mental health. The principal at his school told me, *"School is like a giant family and people fight sometimes."* How do you say that to a 9-year-old who tells you he wishes he was dead?

We got a lot of kickback from the community for taking our children out of the school and were told that *people like you* are the reason small-town schools close. Some still won't talk to us because they really don't know or understand what our boys went through. I feel like we were ostracized completely from our community, but I'll do whatever it takes to advocate for my children.

Our twins had a phenomenal teacher early on, Miss M., and she also happened to be their teacher for 3 years in a row. She set up the classroom in a way that allowed all children to succeed. There were minimal distractions and little rubber bouncers at every desk. She also turned all the desks around so they couldn't rummage inside them. She was strict, but the boys benefited from knowing exactly what was going to happen and when. She gave them body breaks and would organize the information for them so they could easily understand it. She never, not once, said anything negative about my kids. She built on their strengths and found ways to shore up weaknesses without any shame. We were really sad when they no longer had her as their teacher. The boys would not be where they are today had they not had her during those pivotal years. Miss M. will always be fondly remembered by all of us.

The last set of parent/teacher interviews I attended was several years ago and all we received were negative comments from every teacher except for one. Lucas and I were deflated and near tears by the time we got to the last teacher, so I sent him to go look at the school clothing order. I approached the very last teacher, Mr. Biccum, with trepidation, and surprisingly, his words were something I was not expecting to hear. *"You have a really good kid. He has his good days and bad days, but he is an excellent kid."* I fought to hold back my tears. This was the *only* positive comment received that evening. I still regret sending Lucas away and robbing him of the opportunity to experience hearing that positivity himself.

It was through the journey with my kids and understanding their own uniqueness and intricacies, that I discovered the reasons for my own unexplained behaviours. For as long as I can remember, I have always had texture issues with food, which heavily impacted my diet. Certain social situations and eye contact made me uncomfortable and I never felt like I fit in. I have a heightened awareness of sounds which can contribute to distraction, difficulty concentrating, and irritability at times. I dislike people in my personal space and close contact where rapid movements like tapping or quick brushing of the skin occur. This doesn't make for a very snuggly, touchy-feely mom which I often feel bad about. I describe myself as a *sensory hider*. Having three children who are sensory seekers who require excess stimuli or creating those stimuli to regulate means that we clash big time, each and every day which leads to arguments and difficulty remaining in the same space together.

My husband and I were both diagnosed with ADHD in our thirties after our children's diagnoses. Growing up, we both experienced intense feelings that lead to unhealthy coping mechanisms for our undiagnosed anxiety, depression, and ADHD symptoms. With better understanding and treatment we both developed healthier coping mechanisms.

One of my biggest fears has always been that our boys would develop addictions too. This has motivated me to access different therapies, groups, and resources, and speak openly and honestly with them. I want to give them as many positive tools as possible to help them cope with the challenges life throws at them.

The women in my family taught me that it really does take a village to raise a child and you do whatever it takes to advocate for your kids. I wish they would have also spoken about how hard motherhood can be.

Keeping our children alive is the easy part but the fear of loss, difference, acceptance, loneliness, and isolation while trying to keep them safe, confident, and loved in today's world is incredibly hard. I also learned early in my motherhood journey that it's so very important that a child has someone who loves them without judgement and can be their safe haven. My boys were fortunate to have both my Oma Elly and their Grandma Elaine as their safe havens when they were alive.

If you are a parent with a child who doesn't fit inside of the *normal box*, I would encourage you to find a parent support group, advocate for early intervention if you can, and access as many support services, both public and private, for your child. It sometimes feels like you have a bullseye on your back when you're constantly speaking up and advocating for your kids, but that's the price you pay to get the necessary support and intervention for your children. I am most proud of myself for always being their advocate and as long as I am their mother, I will continue to be their advocate. My hope is that they become comfortable enough to embrace their uniqueness, take pride in their strengths and who they are, and continue to share their kindness, compassion and support with others. I hope they can forgive their mistakes and find whatever it is that fills their cup.

"We aren't Born Mothers. We Become Mothers."

I had the opportunity a few years back to interview renowned Canadian child psychologist and speaker, Dr. Jody Carrington, as a guest on the *Strong as a Mother* conversation series. The moment someone said to me, "You have to check out Dr. Jody, you'll love her!" I immediately found her Facebook page, watched a video she did, laughed my ass off and felt this spark ignite inside of me as she boldly and bravely just told it like it was.

During the pandemic, it was Dr. Jody's early morning coffee chats that brought laughter and lightness not only into my life but into the lives of thousands and thousands of women. She has this way of making you feel seen, heard and valued, like an old childhood best friend. It took 10 seconds of courage for me to hit the send button on my email to her team asking her to join me for a podcast conversation during the pandemic. When I opened the email response and read that she'd accepted my invitation I was over the moon excited and that time spent interviewing her will always be one of the most memorable experiences of my life. She said something during our interview that stuck with me and changed the way I viewed myself and my journey as a mother. She said, 'We aren't born mothers. We become mothers.'

It's so, so true, yet we all expect ourselves to get it right on the first try: conception, the birth, breastfeeding, sleep schedules, time outs, and the teenage years. The truth is, we are always in the *becoming* stage of motherhood with each new milestone, adversity, joy, and sorrow we experience. We are on a life-long ride through motherhood that takes us through peaks and valleys, with the opportunity for self-reflection and growth that requires gentleness with ourselves to make it through.

My growth process as a mother has also been a grief process, and I work hard to give myself grace on difficult days. When life gets overwhelming, we tend to lose sight of the joy and easily take for granted the little things that we are so fortunate to be able to experience with our loved ones. Living in gratitude isn't always the easiest when you're faced with fifty loads of laundry, dishes piled high in your sink, a tantrum-throwing toddler, or a baby that just won't sleep. It's ok not to feel grateful for every single moment of this journey, it doesn't mean that you aren't grateful.

When we become a mother, we lose a part of ourselves. It just has to be that way and no matter what anybody says, once you're a mother, you're different and there's no going back to your *old self* - that person no longer exists. There are most definitely aspects of her that exist, but not the same version. We lose autonomy, independence, a free schedule, time for ourselves, and sleep, we lose *a lot* of sleep.

We also don't know what cards we are going to be dealt at the motherhood table. We can only guess at the skills needed to raise this little human that's growing inside of us. We definitely need patience, empathy, intuition, selflessness, and kindness. The list of motherhood requirements and expectations is endless.

Every woman has a mother, but not every woman becomes a mother. We are raised as women with the expectation to bear children. Some believe the root of that expectation is biblical others would suggest physiological but nonetheless, if you're a woman, you're expected to become a mother. It's almost assumed that your path will lead you there and if it doesn't, there's a path of judgement and questions awaiting you.

I knew that in writing this book, I wanted to include all versions and lenses of motherhood - including those who have not yet or may never become mothers. It's almost taboo to talk about - childless women. They carry a burden of expectation from society that's a heavy one and one that you cannot fully understand unless you've walked in those shoes.

One of my most treasured, life-long friends, Chantelle, is not a mother. She grew up in the same small rural community as me, and we attended Kindergarten through Grade 12 together. She's one of those friends you can have a coffee or a phone chat with after not seeing or speaking to for months, and it feels like you didn't even skip a beat. Chantelle's been with me through the tumultuous and adventurous years of adolescence, the early years of marriage and the hard times of divorce. I love her dearly and admire her tenacity and commitment to her passion, navigating waters in society that are not typically considered a *woman's world.* I have so much respect for the amount of dedication it's taken her to get where she is today, and it hasn't been easy. Reaching out to her and asking her to be a part of this book did present some anxiety and uncertainty for me. I did not want her contribution to come across as the token childless story but rather, share a side of womanhood that's not talked about nearly enough: what happens when you don't become a mother?

Taking Up Space

CHANTELLE MEDERNACH

Women are so powerful and we know that. When we are in a community and in a collective as women, we can do anything. Raising families and being part of a community was meant to be done collectively and western culture has really dropped the ball on that. It does take a village to raise a child and for the most part, I think we are really missing that in our culture. Some of my fondest memories as a child are of family reunions, slow pitch tournaments, family weddings, and any time our extended family gathered together. I had many older cousins to look up to and grew up surrounded by aunties. I didn't realize that not everyone had 30 first cousins as I did. I was the youngest of four children and quite a bit younger than my older three siblings so I definitely had the advantage of being able to do things that other kids probably didn't get to do.

I was a very active little girl, watched sports often, and loved being outside. I remember being in girl guides and looking through the badges being excited about being able to do things other than "bake" to get the badges. I was very shy but could read before I went into Kindergarten and that was largely because my siblings read to me all the time. I read in school and had quite a bit of knowledge but was nervous to speak. One of my core childhood memories was when I was in Grade 1 and we were asked to do a presentation on animals. I had chosen to do my presentation on kittens, but our teacher couldn't really hear me well and she shamed me for not speaking up. In Grade 2, we were colouring and I got sent to the back table to colour because I wasn't colouring properly. The back table was for the kids who needed help at school, which was so embarrassing for me. When I reflect on that experience now, I think how badly could a child possibly be colouring to have to be segregated from the rest of the class for remedial colouring? We are conditioned early to be people pleasers and to gain acceptance and approval from others.

My mom was a teacher so I spent quite a bit of time at the school with her while she was finishing her marking and planning. She was a hard worker and I wish I could have half of the energy she's had all of her life. She has raised a family, worked full-time, and planted a garden. She did it all. She was the anchor of not only our family but our extended family. *She got shit done.* Our relationship was a bit stormy at first when I was younger. I felt like I couldn't relate to her or that she couldn't relate to me. I wouldn't say she was the classic nurturing mother but is being nurturing the standard measurement of being a good mother? My mother has been there for both of her parents' deaths, and two sisters' deaths. She's always there, without question. Isn't it ironic how our relationships with our parents improve as we get older and we see them through our adult eyes?

I spent so much time at the school with my mom when I was little, so I suppose it was inevitable that I become a teacher. I also considered being a vet or a lawyer but was leery of the time commitment. Ironically, I'm 43 and still in school working on my PhD. When I graduated high school, I recall that I wanted to become a teacher if I could be a high school physical education teacher. I had a strong desire to coach and there was a time I wanted to be a sports psychologist, but in my first year of university, I had a conversation with a sports psychology professor, who thought it would be difficult for me to get into that field because I wasn't an Olympian or playing a professional sport. I was playing women's softball at a high level, but it wasn't enough for people to *take me seriously*. It was after that conversation that I decided the teacher's path was for me. The irony is that I went on to get a master's degree and took many classes in advanced sports psychology. I coach competitive volleyball at the college level and my dissertation for my PhD is on female athlete mental health. I could've become a sports psychologist and looking back I realize how one opinion from that professor had such an influence on a huge life decision. As women, I think we are taught to not question things, especially if it comes from a man in a position of power or someone we perceive as an expert.

I have worked with female athletes for over twenty years now. I have male counterparts that like coaching women, and some are really good at it, and some are not, but I think they enjoy coaching women because they say they're so coachable. As a female coach, what I see, are female athletes who are receptive to coaching because they come in thinking that they're not enough and think they need to change themselves. In my experience, women are definitely more people pleasers than men, so it makes sense that we are more coachable.

I've been in a male-dominated career most of my whole life; as women, most of us are. I was once at a national-level coaching awards ceremony and an award recipient mentioned that we should be thanking the wives and families for supporting us as coaches because they have to sacrifice so much time. He said, "So I hope that you all do that, thank your wives." I remember thinking, *did he just say that?* I was the only female coach in a room full of men and I looked over to my own significant other, who is an extremely supportive man that has also sacrificed for my career, but is not a wife and I felt so angry; angry and embarrassed for the coach on the stage, for my significant other and for society.

In most professions, there's this underlying assumption that if you have kids, especially small kids, you're a liability. Either you're not going to stay committed that long to the job or you'll be inadequate because your family and kids will be your priority. Somewhere along the line, it is implied for women that being a mother slows us down in our careers, so we have to choose to be one or the other. Mothers who work outside of the home need to prove they can win at both motherhood and their careers.

Society expects women to have children at a certain age, otherwise, you might be deemed an *old mom*. It's a double-edged sword because after you're past your childbearing years people ask why you don't have kids. They assume there's something wrong with you or maybe you couldn't sustain a relationship or gave everything to the career, or *gasp* are too selfish or cold to be a mother. There are always assumptions. So you're not trusted because you don't have kids, but earlier on in your career, you're not trusted because you do have kids. Again, it serves society to do that. When is a man most likely to commit, marry, and become a father? He does these things when he feels financially secure and stable, yet we don't afford women that option when it comes to being a mother, because our biological clocks are ticking.

I would be so rich if I had a dollar for every time someone said something to me about being childless. It might have been well-intentioned, but it's completely rude or inappropriate. *"So you're going to be a career woman Chantelle? That's what you're going to do?"* I remember thinking, what a rude thing to say. It's not just rude to me but to all women, because basically, the insinuation is that you can be a career woman or you can have a family, but you can't have them both successfully. So any woman who works outside of the home and has a family is somehow *less than* and any woman who doesn't have a career or stays at home with her family is also considered to be less than. Would anybody ever say that to a man who doesn't have kids? Would a man ever hear, "I guess you're just going to be a career man then, hey?"

Women can move mountains and make things happen if we want to, but the one obstacle in our way is judgement. And often, we are doing the judging of each other. Unfortunately, as women, we are sold this bill of goods - we can have it all, all the time, concurrently, if we just try hard enough and do what needs to be done. We buy into the belief that we are fundamentally flawed as women.

When it comes to women that don't have kids, we want to know why they don't have kids. Are they a "career woman"? Are they infertile? Are they someone who just decided they don't want to have kids? If I am questioned as to why I don't have kids and I say that I have a reproductive disease and have had miscarriages I feel it immediately makes people feel and think a different way about me compared to if I said "I just don't think motherhood is for me." God forbid that because the judgement is fierce if you've decided you just don't actually want children. *"You don't want to be alone for the rest of your life Chantelle. Who is going to look after you when you're older?"* How many elderly people do you know who are being looked after by their kids? Western culture has it backwards, and we put our elderly loved ones into institutions, not into our own homes. There is no guarantee that if you have kids, you'll be looked after by them.

When I got married, I thought it felt like a partnership, however, things that I wanted to do were just not going to be possible if I stayed in that marriage. It became apparent that we had too many conflicting belief systems about things and I knew I didn't want to try and save our marriage by having children. We divorced and it was not easy. I went on to get a master's degree at the age of 31 and later moved out of the province. It was easy for people to say we split because he wanted kids and I didn't. That theme followed me for a long time and it was the wrong narrative, but there wasn't anything I could do to change what people thought. I had to work to let go of all of that.

During my marriage, I didn't know at the time that I had a reproductive disease. When I finally did get into a relationship where I felt safe to explore having a family, I had stage 4 endometriosis and had emergency surgery. I had a miscarriage. I remember having a conversation with a male gynecologist expressing how difficult it was to even work when I had my cycle and he responded by saying he couldn't really relate because he didn't know what it was like to have a period - exactly, you don't. In my early thirties, I wanted to investigate freezing eggs as I didn't have a partner at the time and felt the pressure of my biological clock ticking. Again, a male gynecologist brushed it off with a chuckle, telling me that I didn't need to do that as I was still young. I have developed so much anger toward the medical system and felt unheard - always felt brushed off.

IVF is financially prohibitive, mentally and physically exhausting and even dangerous to health for women who go that route to have children. It's approximately $20,000.00 for one round depending on where you are located and most people need three to four cycles if they are even able to conceive that way. It feels like it's a penalty to pay for not being able to have kids. Having to make that financial commitment, sacrificing a down payment on a mortgage on a home just to be able to hold on to a string of hope that you just may still be able to have your own biological children. I can't help but think, if this was something that fundamentally affected males, would they have to "pay up" or would it be rolled into healthcare coverage? I feel as a society we have this collective expectation that women should just keep trying and keep trying and keep trying, at all costs, to have children. I'm fortunate now to be with a man who acknowledges and understands that having a child could come at the cost of an irreversible health condition for me and we may not be willing to risk that.

There was a part of my life where having kids didn't resonate with me, and a large part of it was because I wanted to feel safe, solid and secure myself before bringing a child into this world. Through my own personal journey, I've learned to be more aware of what I say to other people because I know how one comment, although well-intentioned, can really hurt someone. When we find ourselves in a place of judgement it's usually because we feel there is something lacking in ourselves. People are who they are and we either accept who they are and have them part of our life or they're not part of our life.

I have so many more options and opportunities than my mother or grandmother had and hope the next generation of women will have more than I had. Was I ready to be a teacher when I became one? No. Was I ready to become a coach? No. I had to learn the skills along the way and I had opportunities to grow professionally and personally. Is anyone ever ready to become a mother? No one has it all right, all of the time. I'm most proud of gaining awareness and being accepting of others. I recognize how hard things can be for people and I just want others to be seen and accepted for who they are. The less competition we have with one another, and the more understanding we have for one another, the more we will thrive.

Earth Angels

There are times in our lives when we meet people who are *earth angels*. These people come into our lives for a reason, a season, or maybe even a lifetime, and leave an imprint on our hearts that can never be forgotten. When I think about my godmother, Barbara, a courageous woman who navigated divorce, and single motherhood, and then bravely and boldly spent seven years of her life trying to heal her body from ovarian cancer, I think about how despite all of her struggles, she never harboured bitterness or resentment. I cannot recall ever seeing her in a bad mood and I always admired her ability to look on the bright side.

Barbara had the most beautiful voice and could sing any harmony effortlessly. When I was a young girl, the two of us sang together in our church Christmas carol festival. The name of the song we sang was *Let There be Peace on Earth* - very fitting for someone who despite all of her struggles, always continued to share her love and gifts with others.

In the week leading up to the day she took her last breath, I sat by her side in her hospice bed, soaking up every last bit of time I could spend with her. I offered to do some journaling with her, leaving a small memoir of written words of remembrance for her children and family. She had a way with words and as I re-read the journalling I did with her at that time, I can now see how the gift of spoken and written word runs in our family. Although she'll never read this book, she's one of the foundational forces of love behind this book and I wanted to include an excerpt of the spoken words she shared with me just days before she passed away.

> "I am so grateful in my life to have been loved by so many and to have been able to give my love to so many. I've been told that I have so much strength but it comes from those who love and encourage me to do what I need to do. A good friend recently asked me what she could do for me as she felt helpless. I told her it wasn't what she could do for me but what she has done for me all of my life - loved me unconditionally and accepted me for who I am. That is what I wish for all of you. I wish that no matter what life brings you, you remember how much you are loved and that you thank God for all of the blessings you have been given in your life. The best thing you can do for each other is to be kind. The more compassionate and loving you are, the more you'll receive and your life will be full of everything you need. Just look for it, it's there." - Barbara Lepitzki, January 19th, 2009

When someone we love dies, there's this deep ache in our hearts and immense heaviness in our chests that we cannot quench. Our days following the loss are filled with a thick, dense fog and it almost feels like we are living in some sort of an alternate reality as we try to digest life without our loved one. The depth of our grief for someone we've lost runs parallel to the depth of our love for them. We cannot have one without the other; there's no grief without love and no love without grief. I feel so blessed to have been loved by Barbara and miss her immensely. I find myself being swallowed up by the waves of grief some days when I think about what life may have been like had her time not been up at the tender age of 49. I think about how much she would've loved the grandchildren, nieces and nephews she was never able to meet. I also think about the ripple effect and waves of impact she created during her life. We can focus on the life of our loved ones, or we can focus on their death.

Barbara's humble character and unwavering dedication to her boys and her family remind me of another earth angel who came into my life when I was just a young teacher. Her name was Sherry. She was a fellow teacher with a strong passion to make an impact in the lives of the students she taught. She's also one of the most beautiful, selfless, empathetic, and caring mothers I know. I was fortunate to teach all four of her children during my teaching career and each of them most definitely carries a strong piece of their mama. Sherry is humble, so very humble. She struggled with being part of this book because she didn't think that her story was worthy enough or that her struggles were big enough, to make it into an inspirational book about motherhood. Sherry exudes the unconditional love mothers have for their children; the love that never wanes. I am just one of many, many women who've been inspired by Sherry and I am so thankful that she decided to step into a new level of vulnerability and share her story of becoming a mother.

Life with Michael

SHERRY BOYLE

I was born in 1959 and as the oldest of four children, I always seemed to naturally gravitate to the role of caregiver. I recall being as young as seven years old doing family chores and caring for my younger siblings. As a young girl I had hoped to play the piano and figure skate, but that just was not an option as responsibilities on the farm came first. Books became my escape, as I could not take part in after-school sports and activities and I became a 'bookworm'. My parents did not encourage me to attend university as their vision for my life was simple; get married, have kids, and stay home. They wanted me to stay safe and university life was "filled with drugs and parties." Fortunately for me, the principal of our high school saw my potential and encouraged me to pursue education. After graduating, I went to university and in 1981 I convocated with a Bachelor of Education degree, with Honours.

I got married during my last year of university and taught for eight years before I became a mother. My first pregnancy was a breeze and the birth of my first son, Michael, was quite easy. He was my first baby so of course I did not know what to expect. Initially, while his Apgar scores were fine, there were certain physical features that were a bit different, and nursing was not going well. The doctor and nurses seemed to feel something was *off* but did not communicate that to us. It seemed as though they did not know how to approach us with their concerns, so instead, they tended to ignore us as I struggled to try to figure out what to do with this newborn sleepy baby who would not eat.

One evening a nurse came in around midnight and saw that I was struggling. She said to me, "You know, Sherry, God gives special kids to special people." I wanted to respond with, "What the hell does that mean?" as I found her words strange and unexpected. No one had mentioned to us that there was something *wrong* with Michael. I knew he wasn't nursing well, and no one was helping me, but I had no clue what she was talking about.

The next morning another nurse came in and I will forever be grateful to her. She is what I call an *earth angel* as she saw my tears, acknowledged my concerns, gave me a hug, and helped us sort things out finally. We would soon find out that everything was not normal or typical at all with Michael.

When Michael was six days old we travelled to Saskatoon to see a geneticist. At that time, we were told that there were three possibilities of conditions; the most severe being Rubinstein-Taybi Syndrome which involved physical and mental delays, but the doctor reassured us that he did not think that was the case. We were told to take him home, treat him like a *normal* baby and return in six months.

Prior to becoming a mother, I thought I was somewhat of a baby whisperer. I was good with any baby and could always soothe them, but that certainly was not the case with my own son. He was a *failure to thrive* baby and breathing was not easy for him. Nursing never was successful. It would take an hour and a half for him to drink two ounces of formula. This was exhausting for him and he was not gaining weight. I internalized his struggles and thought it was all my fault. I was sure I must have been doing something wrong. There were many nights that I cried and cried because I could not help him. I lost so much confidence in my ability to care for him.

At six months, we returned to the geneticist and received an official diagnosis of Rubinstein Taybi Syndrome (RTS). It is a relatively rare syndrome, appearing in 1 in 300,000 births. The diagnosis was based on observations of physical and behavioural characteristics. I asked the Saskatoon geneticist for information and was told that there were very few studies available, so we went home with nothing to read, and very little support, which ended in more frustration.

At our third geneticist appointment in Saskatoon, I was adamant that they give us some written information on RTS as I was only blaming myself for everything. Not one doctor, besides the geneticist, that we were dealing with, had heard of RTS. Finally, the geneticist gave me a few pages of information, warning me that I would find the information alarming. I devoured the few sheets given to us and copied them to share with any professionals that would be working with Michael.

In those few sheets, I found mention of a support group in Texas. Thankfully, there was a phone number, and I made a call to the head of the support group who turned out to be the most loving, caring woman - another *earth angel* in our life. She spent over an hour on the phone with me, sharing everything she could, promising me to send information she had collected from other parents of RTS kids. I was so grateful to finally understand Michael's syndrome, and I began to build my confidence as a mother and address his needs.

When Michael was six months old my maternity leave was over, and financially I needed to return to work. As much as I loved teaching I was devastated and anxious about leaving Michael with a babysitter. Who could I find that would care for him and acknowledge his needs? Once again one of our earth angels emerged. Michael's caregiver was a confident woman, the mother of four amazing kids herself, and she was exactly what he and I both needed. She took Michael in, so I could return to work, and he quickly became part of her family as well.

Once Michael passed the precarious infant stage and survival was not the main goal, he began to smile and interact. He was incredibly cute, happy, and so friendly! The usual toddler and young child milestones were delayed, but they were achieved. He began to walk at age 3, talk at age 6, and was potty trained at age 8 or 9. Each achieved milestone was met through determination and patience, and each was hugely celebrated!

At home and at daycare Michael's needs were met and understood, but I worried about what life would be like for him in school. In his early school years, Michael, with the help of a teacher's aide, was easily integrated into the class with his peers. There were many teachers and support aides that strived to develop a program that met his needs and interests, and under their care, he thrived. He even learned how to read in grade one at the same stage as his peers. Unfortunately, through his school years, there have also been a few people that would not take the time to acknowledge and understand him. Fortunately for Michael, they were few.

When Michael was about to enter grade five, we moved to the farm, resulting in a change of schools which I was anxious about. I was able to go in and talk to Michael's new class. I also asked his previous classmates to make postcards for Michael's new classmates from their point of view. The postcards were frank and to the point, but loving as well, and it was obvious that his previous peers knew him well. As I was speaking to his new classmates, I spied one young man in the back row sprawled over his desk watching me suspiciously. When I asked for questions, his was simple, "Is this something we can catch from Michael?" When I responded and explained Michael's syndrome a little more carefully, he said aloud to the entire class, "Ok, who is on Michael's bus? If anyone on that bus is giving Michael a hard time you let me know!"

When Michael returned to the room a bubbly girl with the bluest of eyes bounced up to Michael and said, "Hello, Michael, my name is Kristen, but you can call me KK. I will be your new best friend!" and to this day she has lived up to that promise. He had the honour of having a special dance with her at her wedding. She made sure he attended their class reunion, and she was one of his first visitors when he was in the hospital with a broken leg. She has been another earth angel for our family.

With the move in schools came another couple of more *earth angels* in the form of an amazing educational associate by the name of Marilee, and the school librarian, Mrs. P. Marilee is a special woman with a gift of connecting with children and became Michael's anchor during his school years and beyond as he felt safe and acknowledged in her presence. Mrs. P gave Michael the job of getting the library ready in the morning and tidying it up at the end of the day and he would help return books to their proper places.

The transition to high school was particularly difficult for Michael as the cognitive and social-emotional gap between him and his peers grew more obvious and difficult to accommodate. During this time, it was more challenging for some teachers to provide meaningful inclusion for Michael. Some were wonderful, and others did not make the effort or the time. The school did provide alternative learning opportunities, and in this group, Michael made new and lifelong friends. We appreciated the many teachers, aides, librarians, janitors, and peers who took the time every day to acknowledge, accept, connect with, and listen to Michael. Those people made Michael's preschool to grade 12 amazing years.

In 2007, Michael proudly stood on the graduation stage with those new friends he had made back in grade five. There were many tears in the crowd as we watched him walk across the stage, and they were not all mine. After graduation from our small local high school, Michael went on to attend a school-based program for special needs young adults in a larger community one hour away. He attended that program for two and a half years. Presently, Michael is in an amazing group home thirty minutes from our home, and he attends a day program as well that is run by the same association. He has made many new friends and is greatly supported but he still requests to come home every weekend, as family is truly so important to him. In the last year, he has become an uncle to a beautiful little niece and is loving that relationship as the two of them have a very special bond.

Life took a turn for our family when Michael was in his final year of the special needs classroom. I was 49 years old at the time and noticed that I had developed a red, swollen area on my left breast. Breast cancer did not run in my family. There was no lump and I had none of the risk factors associated with cancer. My doctor treated me for mastitis, which seemed rather strange for my age and the redness and the pain disappeared.

I knew that the area still did not look quite right so at my next appointment I was booked for a mammogram a few months later. If you have ever gone through a mammogram and the technician calls you back for a second, then a third test, then an ultrasound, you know that sickening feeling that something is very wrong. Then there is the suggested diagnosis, the biopsy, and the gut-wrenching confirmation that you have cancer. It is a feeling you never, ever forget.

Although the tumour was quite large, I could not feel it. The oncologist and surgeon explained that it was an unusual shape and consistency, rather like a sponge with tentacles. It was growing quickly and aggressively. At first, they were concerned I might have inflammatory breast cancer, a very dangerous breast cancer, but after the biopsy, they determined it was not inflammatory breast cancer; rather my body was having a very inflammatory reaction to the cancer. My body was sending me a message that something was very wrong.

As it was a very aggressive form of Cancer, they wanted to do chemo first to slow the tumour's growth, then radiation, followed up with a mastectomy. My response to the doctors was "Do what you have to do, I still have four kids in school." Michael was in his special program, and my other three children were in grades 12, 10, and 6.

I went into panic mode wondering about what Michael would do without me in his life.

No one would ever know him as I did. I tried writing down an "All About Michael Booklet" for whoever would be caring for him should I not survive the cancer, but I just could not do it. It was too overwhelming. I remember saying to my mother, "Ok, I have a plan. The plan is, *I do not get to die. I really can't die*. I need to know that Michael is in a safe place. I need to see my last child graduate and all of my kids still need me." And so, my cancer fight began.

I went through eight chemo treatments, two different types. Every three weeks another blessed *earth angel*, my friend, Diane, would drive me two hours for my chemo treatment and then home again. She wrote notes for me during my doctor appointments and held my hand through the chemo. Diane was a working mother of five children who had a lot on her own plate, but she gave me so much support and to this day I am eternally grateful.

Once radiation started, I was able to drive myself back and forth to treatment for fifteen days. I would see the kids off for school, drive in for my treatment, and then be home before Michael was home. I wanted life to be as normal as possible for Michael and his siblings. Following the radiation, I had a complete mastectomy, a hysterectomy, and five years of estrogen blockers. My second chemo treatments were rough. The pain in my joints was intense, and I still have some lasting joint and nerve damage from that. The estrogen blocker was also very rough on my joints. I recall one night crying because I could not get into our tub, it was just too painful.

I turned 50 during my first round of chemo. A friend of mine held a surprise party; my first birthday party ever! I was overwhelmed by the love and support from these wonderful women. As word spread of my diagnosis, I was amazed by the many letters, phone calls, cards, and kindness from neighbours and family. People dropped off food and offered our kids rides to their activities. We had a village of people willing to support and care for us. It opened my eyes to the importance of reaching out to others who are going through a rough time. We are here to support and care for others in need. Kindness and caring are so easy but mean so very much. Dr. Jody Carrington often uses the quote by Ram Daas, "We are all just walking each other home." I too believe that caring and connection are vital for all of us.

As difficult as the cancer treatments were, I felt a great deal of anxiety when they were all done, and I was no longer going to the cancer clinic. This is anxiety no one seems to talk about, but I know other cancer survivors I've spoken to feel the same. While I was going through treatments, I felt like we were doing something to destroy the cancer. I had a team of professionals supporting me and then it was all over. The professional support was gone, and there would be no follow-ups, except with my family doctor, and I found it to be scary. I would question every weird feeling in my body. Is the cancer back? How will I know? Am I *really* ok? Why does my body still hurt so much? Shouldn't I feel more relieved, more grateful? Then there was also a feeling of survivor's remorse that I dealt with. Why did I make it through when others I knew and cared for did not?

I consider myself incredibly lucky to have survived cancer, but at the time, I did not feel that the journey was in any way a "blessing" to me. I had already learned enough life lessons through Michael's journey and motherhood. At the time, I did not feel that any lessons were learned through having cancer, but I was wrong.

Six years after my cancer diagnosis I went with my daughter to pick out her Grad dress and suddenly I started crying. I was unable to stop, recalling my fears that I may not have been there to experience that day with her. I have had the opportunity to walk down the aisle with my son as he married the love of his life and did the same with our daughter this summer. When I held my very first grandchild, I again thanked the Lord for that moment. While I would have loved those moments even before cancer, I do not believe that the intensity of my gratitude and emotions would have been the same. I try not to take life for granted. Each day is a gift and because of the cancer, I have learned to appreciate life more.

Having cancer also pushed me to think more clearly about Michael's future. I wanted to ensure he was in a supportive environment with staff that know and understand his needs. It made me acknowledge that I cannot always be there for Michael. He will outlive me. I needed to let go a little to allow and to trust others, staff, friends, and family to care for him.

Life with Michael has taught us so much. No one talks about the grief you go through as a parent of a special needs child. You still have your child, but you lose so many of the dreams you may have had for that child. The fact that he knows and sees those dreams not happening is so hard to witness as a mother. People sometimes think that because Michael's IQ level is lower, that he does not have the same feelings or dreams as everyone else, or that he doesn't realize how his life is at times limited. He does experience the same feelings and he has the same dreams, but he does not always have the maturity to think them through rationally.

Everyday Michael sees his siblings accomplishing things he cannot do. Every day he sees friends and others doing things he will not do. He will not get his driver's license. He will likely not marry, and if he does it will not be with the independence experienced by others. He will not have children. He will not be a doctor, a teacher, an astronaut, a power ranger, a cowboy, or a paleontologist. He will not achieve so many of his dreams and it breaks his heart and mine each time a dream is crushed.

I heard a parent once say that if they could take away their child's syndrome, they would not do it because the child has brought so much into their life. I agree Michael has brought us so much joy and understanding to us, but if I could take away his syndrome, and the pain, and frustration it brings him, I would in a heartbeat. I would do that for him, not for me. I would do it so he could experience being independent and so that he could experience some of those dreams and wishes he has.

From the time he was born, we knew it was our job to bring Michael all the happiness in life we could. We have made it our goal to travel with him and to give him as many experiences as we can. Through it all, Michael has taught me patience, unconditional love, the importance of listening, kindness, and acknowledging others. His capacity to learn, to dream, his empathy, his determination, and his attention to life's small delights all inspire me to be a better person. I have learned to slow down and appreciate family and life.

On the flip and honest side, Michael is stubborn, not always realistic, and can lash out with anger when frustrated, anxious, confused, scared, hurt, or not feeling seen or heard. It can be exhausting and draining to meet his physical, developmental, and emotional needs. There were times in his twenties when he would rage and trash his room and the house. It can be a lonely life as so much time is required and dedicated to caring for Michael. At times I am exhausted and tired and know I need to take care of myself, but when do I fit that it in? Again, well-meaning people comment and say, "I just don't know how you do it, I could not do what you do for Michael." Interesting perspective as I did not ask for this, I did not choose this, I did not sign up for this, but I love him with my whole being and I will stand in front of a train for him. I will give him a voice. I will protect and support him. He is my child and I am his mother.

Michael is our *forever child.* He still needs us to bathe him, clean him, help him dress, to explain life to him, and be there for him. It is a lifelong commitment of love, patience, acknowledgment, and understanding. I am able to get through the hard days or rough moments by telling myself, "This too shall pass. This is a moment that will pass." and then I have to let it go. When Michael has had a bad day and is remorseful, I remind him that a good sleep and a new day will make things better. The past is gone, it is history, and we are granted a new day and a fresh start.

Years ago, I started taking Michael to see Laura when she opened her BodyTalk practice. At first, I was skeptical, but I literally saw my son "melt' in front of my eyes. I had never seen Michael so completely relaxed. That experience encouraged me to take a closer look at Michael, myself, our relationship, and how this modality of BodyTalk might make a difference in our lives. I have since taken my BodyTalk Fundamentals 1 & 2 class, and MindScape, looking to add more knowledge and tools to my tool belt to work with both Michael and myself. I have also taken my level 1, 2, and practitioner's course in Reiki. I initially started to take these courses to help Michael, and then I quickly realized that I too benefitted as Michael and I mirror each other, and these alternative healing modalities have brought more balance, awareness, patience, and healing into our lives.

Having Michael in our home has taught our entire family so much about life, love, and empathy. Michael's three younger siblings will not tolerate bullying or the mistreatment of others. They make me so proud. If they see someone who needs help, they will jump right in. They know what it feels like to have a *Michael* in their lives or be a *Michael.* They are incredibly compassionate adults, and will always lead with their hearts. They take the time to acknowledge others: and as a family, we have really learned to communicate better.

My advice to other parents with special needs children is to simply listen and be their voice. Do not beat yourself up. Let the negative moments, yours or theirs, go. Tomorrow is always a new day, a new start, and a new chance. Support and encourage them, but do not immerse them in a bubble, which is what our heart wants us to do to protect them. Trust your intuition, but find support professionals that you trust with your child. In our society, unfortunately, programs for special needs adults are still very lacking. It is improving, but it has a long way to go! Advocate for your child and do not accept something if it doesn't feel right for them.

Like most mothers, I have made some mistakes in life that I wish I could change, but I believe I tried to be the best mother and teacher I could be at the time. When former students contact me and say to me, "you made a difference" it touches my heart deeply. I am proud that when I realized life was getting too much for me physically, emotionally, and mentally I reached out for help. I believe, I was surviving on autopilot for a time, so I was not feeling. I was just dealing. I have changed in the last ten years as I started to explore other modalities for healing the body and mind. I have begun to enjoy nature more and sit in the stillness and the calmness. This is not the trip that I imagined as a mother or planned for my life, and although it has felt lonely at times; it has been beautiful and life-changing.

The Intervention

The path I had personally imagined and planned for my life took a wild turn when I was 32 years old, in a direction that ended in divorce. I was a full-time science teacher, living in a brand new house that my ex-husband had built us, and just two months after moving in, we were talking about separating. Four months later, he had moved out.

It takes two people to enter into a marriage and two people to exit a marriage and the experiences and perspectives of both people are often very different. What I know to be true in my own heart for our experience, is that two people got married who loved each other very much. They were high-school sweethearts and were together for seven years before they married. They travelled together, bought their first house together, and supported each other through careers and new adventures. They brought two beautiful souls into this world, attended funerals of loved ones, and also grieved the loss of a child through miscarriage together. In the midst of all of that, there was pain, anger, resentment, mistakes and personal challenges that both people had to work through, and still continue to work on. From that marriage came two amazing children who, without their parents falling in love at one time, never would've been born to share their hearts and unique gifts with this world.

In the early days of the separation, I had fallen deeply into a dark fog that affected every aspect of my life. I lost my signature spark and zest for life that was the essence of who I was. Prior to this experience, I can say that I never really understood depression. I now know very intimately what depression feels like. Although I never thought about taking my own life, I could not seem to drag myself out of the deep grief and fear that came with restarting my life with two small children all on *my own*. The fear of never being able to find someone to love me again was so real. I had always struggled with self-esteem and now it became even more apparent to me the tight grip that self-doubt and limiting beliefs had on me all of my life. I lost 40 pounds, spent a lot of time in bed, lost all motivation for my teaching career, and was lost for what direction I wanted my life to take.

Two good friends of mine saw how deep I was spiralling those first few months after the separation and arranged an intervention weekend for me that changed my life. They booked me a session with a psychologist by the name of Jeanette, a Reiki session, and a BodyTalk session. I had never heard of BodyTalk prior to this but had no energy in me at the time to question anything so just agreed to go along with it.

That intervention weekend is mostly a blur except for a few vivid and memorable details. I remember sobbing the entire time I was on Jeanette's couch, unpacking my broken heart and all of the feelings that came with it, hoping she'd have the answers to how I could fix it all. I remember feeling a very powerful somatic emotional release when the Reiki practitioner's warm hands gently settled on the back of my head. It had been so long since I felt any physical touch and the warmth of her hands felt safe enough for me to let down my guard and release the grief that had been consuming my body. The BodyTalk session left me confused and bewildered but intrigued enough to give it a go again a few months later.

I could never have imagined the impact that weekend would have on my life as it set into play a domino effect. It changed the entire trajectory of my life. A decade later, I still see that same psychologist, Jeanette, on a regular basis and she is one of the foundational pillars of support in my mental health maintenance. In one of our last visits, I genuinely thanked her for everything she's helped me through the last ten years and having both walked similar paths, we shared some kindred tears together.

I have just entered my eighth year as a BodyTalk practitioner, after leaving my full-time job as a teacher shortly after my divorce. By holding space and observing healing shifts for hundreds of clients of all ages over the past number of years, I have been able to see many different versions of myself in those clients. As a practitioner, every session we do for a client offers the potential for healing our own mental, emotional and physical pain. This modality has been a gift not only to my clients but to my family members and to my children as it's offered a whole body approach to healing aspects of our bodymind that hold pieces of our stories that we don't even know still linger. There is no doubt that a powerful connection exists between our minds and our bodies.

I wish I could've seen all of this so clearly back in the darker days as I do now. Would've it been easier to get through that *heavy fog* had I known how it all would've turned out for me and for my kids? We always want to know what lies ahead, so that we can feel *safe,* don't we? I can say, without a doubt, I did not want my marriage to end but it needed to. I don't even know if there would've been an *easier way* for it to end. I cannot imagine what life would've been like had we stayed together, yet it does feel like I've lived two very separate and distinct lives that weave themselves in and out of one another. I do not regret that marriage and have taken so many lessons and beautiful memories with me from it. My ex-husband loved me and I loved him - we just weren't meant to love one another for our entire lives.

To this day, I still continue to work through layers of myself that were formed both before and after the divorce but my ex-husband and I have a relatively decent co-parenting relationship. I know without a doubt that counselling, BodyTalk, physical activity, and everything and everyone that became part of my mental health maintenance plan has contributed to my ability to move beyond the hard emotions and experiences of that difficult time.

Years ago, a woman by the name of Heather called me for a Body-

Talk session as she had heard my name a few times and was experiencing some deep levels of grief she needed some support with. She too needed an intervention that would send her on a new trajectory, and help her work through things her conscious mind didn't even know would be coming her way. Heather started out as a client of mine, but we quickly became friends. It was my privilege to see her grow and evolve in so many ways as she poured herself into healing which would lead her to study to become a BodyTalk practitioner herself. Heather has a natural way of making people feel at ease and is a talented healer with so many gifts to share with others through the healing modalities she's trained in. I have had the opportunity to receive many powerful healing sessions from her and I believe that the divine timing that brought our paths together was purposeful.

Learning to Laugh Again

HEATHER WHITELAW

When I look back to all of the mistakes I made and lessons I learned in motherhood I know without a doubt, I went into motherhood not prepared for any of it. I had no clue what it would be like. I was 20 when I became a mother for the first time. I fell in love at 19, three months later we moved in together and three months later I was expecting our first child. We thought, *well, we'll get married someday but let's have a baby now*; typical thinking for someone so young and has no clue! I don't remember ever thinking about prepping for parenting or thinking about how to physically or emotionally care for a baby. We knew we'd just figure it all out later.

I had four kids between the ages of 20 and 30 and I feel each of them got the survival version of me for many, many years. I don't feel like I was ever really fully present. I do know that my own childhood experiences contributed to my coping mechanisms and programming. My parents got divorced when I was in Grade 1 and there were struggles with alcohol. I didn't always feel like a priority as a child but rather it felt like our parents' social life was often more important. I think when my mother got pregnant with me, she was likely nowhere near ready to be a mother either. I remember spending my entire childhood with my grandparents mostly, not really my parents.

There is one core memory that stands out for me from those years of my childhood when my parents were still together. I was five years old and mom and dad were fighting one night. It was bad and I sat listening to it from the top of my bunk bed and my sister was on the bottom. They were screaming at each other and the energy and the emotion from it all was so intense. My first natural instinct was to try and just *keep the peace* and make sure everyone was ok. I look at my patterns of thinking and my desire to always fix and help others so often in my life and realize, those patterns started very early for me.

I don't even remember how the separation process all went but one day we just packed up and we moved away from my father. Had we met my stepdad prior to that? I'm sure we must have, but I don't even recall that happening. I knew that my mom and him were already together before we moved.

My relationship with my father was limited to a couple of visits a few times a year, some phone calls and letters. It sounds so old school, but that's what we did. We wrote letters to him every couple of weeks. He'd write back and tell us what was going on in his life. It wasn't until I was about 15 years old that I remember him being in my life more. My sister and I would take the bus ourselves and go spend a week here and there or spend some time in the summer with him. When I was 18, I actually got to work with him and that's when I got to know him a bit better; more like a human being, not just as a dad that you saw three or four times a year.

I don't feel that part of my life was overly traumatic, yet I know it greatly impacted me in many ways. I come back to another memory that really did change my relationship with my dad. I was a bratty teenager having to do too many chores at home for mom and when we'd go to dad's place, he'd end up taking that entire time off to spend just having fun with us. I remember saying one day to mom during a fight we had that I thought I wanted to go live with dad. Mom and I were at each other's throats and her response was, *"Oh really? You want to live with your dad? When he and I were separating things and splitting things, 50-50, He wanted to separate you and your sister too. Since you were more like me, he said, you can take Heather and I'll take Darci. He didn't want you, Heather."* Those words stung then and still do today. I don't want to lay blame at all on my mother for sharing that with me, but those are the words that have always made me feel like I wasn't good enough and that in order for someone to love me, I had to work harder to earn it.

From that experience on, I would see little things that would *remind* me that I wasn't as worthy of his love. Dad would call me on my sister's birthday to get her phone number to wish her a happy birthday, but he'd forget my birthday all of the time. They were all just little things, but each felt like one more confirmation that affirmed my belief that he loved me less. Although my logical mind tells me, he loved me just as much, I didn't feel that way. Looking back, I guess I was probably harder to love as my sister would've never rocked the boat and I had a bit more stubbornness in me.

Now, as a parent, I can see things from my childhood through a different lens. I can understand how incredibly difficult it is to be a parent. The older your kids get, it feels like the more complex the problems and struggles get. I would go back to potty training in a heartbeat.

Even when you think you're loving your kids as much as you possibly can, they may see it differently from you and that's difficult. We love our children wholeheartedly, but their experience and perception of their own childhoods or their version of us, as mothers, may be completely different than we would hope it to be. That takes some work on our part; to dig deep and see what's there for us and work through our own self-doubt and guilt. It's heart-wrenching if you ever feel a disconnect from one of your children, and do not know how to fix it.

Like my parents, I too went through a separation and divorce. In reflecting on the breakdown of my own marriage I know that for sure it takes two to get to the end. I think one of the biggest factors for us was communication, or lack thereof, between the two of us. There was always so much stress and we didn't speak each other's love language. There would be little things he would do for me, but that wouldn't be my love language and so I didn't receive the gestures as well as I could have. Like in many relationships, there were insecurities and residual emotions carried over from past experiences that really had an effect on the whole relationship. I remember trying hard not to fight in front of the kids. I never wanted the kids to think that any of our problems were their fault.

For me, feeling emotionally supported by my life partner was a very important aspect of my marriage, so when I didn't feel supported, I started to pull away and put all my energy into the kids versus our family, including my husband. Ironically, that resulted in me emotionally abandoning him as well. I made the conscious choice to do that, which just led to feeling more and more divided.

In the midst of finding myself in troubled marriage waters, my younger sister, Raelene, received her terminal cancer diagnosis. There was so much I needed to do for her and time I wanted to spend with her that it did take away time from healing and working on my marriage. I don't regret any of that. It was a choice I made knowing my sister was dying. I figured he and I would have a future together, but I didn't have a future with her. I probably knew that it was already too late to save the marriage.

I was processing so much grief from losing five close family members in the span of five months, including my little niece and my sister. Because of all of the grief, I booked a BodyTalk with Laura since her name just kept coming up to me. We ended up sitting next to one another at a public event, which I saw as another sign that I needed to book a session with her. My first session was on September 18th, and in that session, she indicated that there was some balancing we needed to do relating to grief towards a man with black hair who thought he would've lived longer than he did. The only man I could think of would've been my father, but I was perplexed about this very clear detail.

I left that session feeling very relaxed and went to work the next day telling my colleague all about it. I later received a phone call from my brother-in-law's mother, concerned that possibly he was sick as she hadn't heard from him in a few days. She asked me if I could go check on my brother-in-law and I just knew I needed to go. As I drove down the driveway to his house, I had this eerie feeling and recall wondering what I would do if I had to call an ambulance for him. What happened is something I couldn't have imagined - I found my brother-in-law deceased at his home. *The "man with the dark hair who thought he'd live longer than he did." Was that him?*

The trauma and PTSD from finding him deceased, added to the grief of losing my sister (his wife) seven months prior, was so intense, with so many layers to work through. I didn't want my kids to have a mom who was in complete trauma mode and non-functional; a mom who wasn't able to hear the phone ring, able to walk outside in the dark by herself, or feeling like she was going to die inside from all of the pent up trauma. I couldn't stay like that so I threw myself into every healing modality I could, sometimes having multiple modalities a day including Reiki, BodyTalk, Access Bars, Craniosacral therapy, and Chakra clearing.

I put so much work into healing myself that I began to feel like myself again. I had forgotten who I was. I forgot that I loved to be barefoot and dance on the grass in the rain. I forgot that I loved to laugh until my stomach hurt. I'm still learning this one, but I think, one of the biggest things is trying to learn to love myself the way I love everyone else. Life is supposed to be about joy, ease and about peace. You don't have to always be in fight or flight mode. You don't always have to make everyone else happy, even though there are days that I still try to! I have this knowing that my body can heal. I've always known it and I think that's what's drawn me into doing this work and training in alternative modalities like BodyTalk and Craniosacral therapy, to help other people. I know that I need to also do my own work, to bring my best self to those I love.

I'm grateful for the partner that I have right now as he reminds me that I am a good mom. He recognizes that I would do anything for all four of my children - something I think at times I wish they could all see too. There are always good memories, but for some reason, it's the negative ones that stay embedded the deepest. I am regretful of the times that I didn't show up as my best self even though I know and understand where I was in those moments as a mother. For example, having three screaming kids on the way home, when everyone's hungry, and you've got to cook supper and you have no help after working all day. Even though I was tired and run down in those moments, there are times when I could've chosen differently. I could have chosen to just take a few deep breaths for 5 seconds to come down just a few notches, but I didn't have coping skills until later on in life when I really dug into doing some work. I was in reaction mode all of the time; constantly in fight or flight.

In the past, I couldn't have been the mom that I am now, because we're always *becoming a mother* and always learning. I recognize that I also couldn't become the mom I am today without going through all of the trauma that led to the healing. I needed to make it a priority for myself. Some people don't do anything and stay stuck in that grief, and I am proud of myself for doing the hard work. We are worthy of putting the work in to find ourselves and heal ourselves. We are worthy of loving ourselves, the way we love others.

Heavy days, Heavy hearts

"You're the worst mom ever."

"I knew I wasn't the favourite one Mom, you love them more than me."

"You want to know what my problem is Mom? My family. Everyone in my family - including you."

"If you put as much effort into being a mom here as you did into your work, things might be different."

"You annoy me when you talk to me. I just want to be left alone."

I know my family can't be the only ones who sling these kinds of stings. There are times it feels like I am the emotional punching bag for my family. It was another heavy week during the pandemic and emotions were all over the place. Truths from temper-tantrum-throwing toddlers to over-emotional teenagers, and an exhausted husband and wife team, all seeking to be seen and heard. Dysregulated nervous systems on high alert seemed to be more common than not these days in our house. It was to be expected though when the whole world had *flipped its' lid*.

We were still in the thick of the pandemic with no sight of any sense of normalcy returning and patience was never my strongest virtue. It felt like we were living in a twilight zone; collectively holding our breath and waiting for our lives to get back to normal, yet fearful that *normal* would never return. It felt like there was no light at the end of the tunnel. Everything as we knew it had changed. Two weeks to flatten the curve in March of 2020 turned into a dangled carrot of how we'd get back to normal, and a divided world filled with fear. I was raised to accept, respect, and never exclude anyone, no matter what. It hurt my heart so much every time I opened my social media scroll or read the news and saw the wedge that was clearly dividing society, workplaces, schools, and families. It was getting wider and wider.

My body was taking the physical brunt of all the collective grief I was feeling. I had developed an inflammatory condition called costochondritis which caused pressure and pain in my chest and upper back and it made breathing difficult. The symptoms, at their peak of intensity, mimicked a heart attack and left me in the emergency room more than once that fall.

I figuratively and literally, could not catch my breath for three months. My lungs felt *squeezed* inside of me from my inflamed sternum and ribcage. My heart literally and figuratively, felt heavy. The first set of x-rays showed possible early onset COPD or chronic lung disease. *How the hell can that be? I've never smoked and I'm only 42 years old.* That information sent me into a spiral of fear as my Oma died of complications from COPD and congestive heart failure. The more I thought about it, the more worked up I got which led to more heaviness and pressure in my chest. That's the power of the connection between our minds and bodies. We can literally manifest physical symptoms through our thoughts. Once I got myself out of my irrational mind, I remembered my background training on consciousness and the role that stress and emotion plays in manifesting physical symptoms in the body. The doctors wanted to rule out everything, so sent me for a CT scan, and other diagnostics. They all came back clear, yet still, the pain and pressure continued.

By this time, I had received a few BodyTalk sessions from different colleagues and each of them had one common theme - grief and feeling out of control. This made complete sense as I developed the condition shortly after having to be the anchor of support for my daughter, who was having an extremely difficult time and many factors in her life challenged her mental health. When I track my physical health all the way back to my teenage years, there's one come thread without doubt: if my mental health is in a fragile state, my body keeps score.

One night, after a particularly difficult couple of days; navigating the latest pandemic rules, juggling toddlers, teenagers, co-parenting with an ex-husband, and everything in between, I felt like my emotions were highjacking our entire house again. My physical body was literally shutting down and I was emotionally all over the place. Chronic pain really does mess with your mind.

I lay beside my husband as we settled into bed with tears in my eyes, exasperation pervading my entire body. Feeling like a complete and epic failure, and incredibly helpless on all fronts, I said to him, "I just don't know how to make things easier for them." His calm, level-headedness at that moment provided a soft place to land once again. He said something to me that I had never considered before. He said, "Laura if your kids are able to solve a problem better than you could have at that age, you're winning at parenthood. *You're doing your job right.*"

Huh, I had never thought of it that way. I was feeling like I wasn't doing a good enough job as a mother. *Good mothers would figure things out.* Maybe it didn't have to be all on me, all of the time? Maybe simply showing them how to walk *through* hard things by giving them healthy tools and having healthy conversations was the best way to help them navigate through the messes in life and solve future problems for themselves as compassionate, critical thinkers.

There was just one problem with that philosophy and it could all be summed up in two small words: mom guilt. I carry this backpack of guilt with me and much of it is filled with the challenges that my older two kids continue to grow through from the divorce and living a life in two separate homes.

Prior to going through my divorce, on a scale of 1-10 of how "hard" divorce is, comparing it to other grief-stricken experiences, I would've rated it quite low on the scale. When I earned my badge as part of the co-parent club my perspective quickly changed. Until you have to balance parenthood by juggling your kids back and forth between an ex, having new people come in and out of their lives, not knowing where they are and what they're doing when they're not with you, and being unable to control any of it, you know how hard divorce can be. I've also come to learn, that on the ACE scale (adverse childhood events), divorce is included as one of the top 10 most difficult traumatic events for children to go through.

When I meet a fellow mom who's part of the *divorce club*, it's like we immediately understand one another on a deeper level. We know how it feels to have to *share* our children. We know the stress that comes with arranging drop-offs and pick-ups, what it feels like to have a quiet house on Christmas morning, or having to blow out candles on a birthday cake a few days after the birthday. We've felt the searing pain of hearing, "I'll just go live with Dad.", during the tumultuous days of teenage rearing.

The first time I met Shannon I just knew she was one of *my people*. She was speaking at an event I was a guest at, and sharing parts of her personal story. Some of what she said, I could very much relate to as a divorcee. There was something about her edgy haircut and stoic presence that I found to be incredibly captivating. In my gut, I knew I just had to befriend this woman, so I reached out to her afterward, letting her know how inspired I was by her story. The rest is history as we became fast friends.

Every girl needs a *Shannon* in their life. The fierce, no B.S. kind of friend that goes for the gusto, and isn't afraid to speak her mind. Also, she has horses. If you know a *horse girl*, you know that they're a whole different breed of women. They're tough AF. When I first met Shannon, I saw her strength. However, the more time I spent with her the more I saw the vulnerable side that turned out to be, like most of us, the foundation of her strength.

I was invited to be a guest presenter at one of her women's wellness horse retreats and it changed my life. Her herd of horses broke me open and reached my darkest wounds in a graceful and beautiful way. The experience really is indescribable. A good friend of mine once told me, "You have to feel it to heal it." Oh did I ever feel it with those horses in her arena that weekend. There were tears and emotional layers shed with those animals by my side that I thought I had already worked through. It turns out, those tears were simply concrete footprints from my past.

I truly believe that I crossed paths with Shannon to teach me that you never have to apologize for being authentically bold, brave, and strong. She is the epitome of standing solidly and proudly in your strength, no apologies needed. I am grateful to have sat with her as she shared vulnerable parts of her healing. She helps other women to see their own worth and strength too.

Victim or Victor

SHANNON DICKEY

I have always felt for some reason that I just didn't belong. I didn't grow up as a "girly-girl" but I've loved animals since before I can even remember. My parents were young when they had me and although I didn't have a particularly sad childhood, they did get divorced when I was 2 years old. My dad stayed living on our family farm and we moved to the city with my mom and lived with my grandparents. I joked that I was like the country mouse and the city mouse, always struggling to fit into both worlds. Although I had so many people around me that loved me, and to this day I consider them incredible blessings, I felt emotionally torn and tugged at.

Looking back now, had my parents never separated I wouldn't have experienced all of the love that I did. At one point I had thirteen grandparents; who can say that? Despite being surrounded by so much love, there was an underlying feeling of not ever really fully belonging. As a teen, I can remember crying every Sunday my dad had to drive me back into the city. I would spend my summers and holidays with my dad but I would miss out on things with my mom's family. At Christmas, I wanted to be able to be with everybody and then there were times when I just didn't want to be with anybody. I would push people and things away, longing to be at peace in the place where I was, but never feeling like I could be. I built emotional walls around me to protect myself. I knew I was loved, yet didn't feel like I belonged.

We had three different last names in our home between all of us. It was a "his, hers and theirs" type of family which at that time wasn't as normal as it is now. I never referred to any of my siblings as *step*. We weren't raised that way, they were simply my sisters and brother. When I was growing up and going to school there was only one other girl in my grade whose parents were divorced like mine. There were so many feelings that I couldn't explain to other kids and that was difficult. I felt isolated in those feelings. At the same time, I don't have any anger toward my parents for divorcing. I can't imagine them together.

I definitely did not grow up dreaming about being a mom. In fact, I never wanted to be a mother. I didn't think I had the ability to be a mom nor did I have the confidence to be. A friend of mine from university and I had agreed we were just going to live like the actors in the sitcom *Friends*. I don't feel bad openly saying that either. Motherhood is painted to be this magical, blissful time for you but we know not too far into it that it's *hard AF*.

I had two boys, both of whom came out of the womb crying. I internalized that so much, feeling like I'd caused their discomfort. My first son had extreme colic and cried non-stop for 6 months. My family all lived a province away so I had no help with this baby that I couldn't help either. I was heartbroken that I couldn't fix things for him and I'd obviously did something wrong to cause this. He was in so much pain and I felt incredibly helpless. It again confirmed my doubts and fears that motherhood wasn't for me. Little did I know that was just the beginning of parenting doubts and feelings of not being able to do enough for them. It doesn't get easier as your kids get older, the hard just changes.

Tyson was maybe three days old and I remember walking through the house with this screaming baby looking over to my then- husband who was on the deck and I felt this instant distance that had surfaced between the two of us. Parenting was overwhelming for me, but I had carried this baby for nine months so I was a bit more prepared for him. My husband had his own challenges that became bigger and magnified when he became a dad. It was apparent from that day on that the kids and I had this bond that felt different from the one we should've all shared as a family.

Tyson stopped crying at about six months, just in time for me to get pregnant again. I was 26, with a 7-month-old thinking, "What the hell am I going to do?" I was going to screw up not just one child, but now two of them. My relationship with my husband was not strong and I didn't have any support. I cried for the first four months of that pregnancy.

As the kids grew older it continued to feel like it was just them and me. We were like the three amigos. I invested my heart and soul into everything I did with them. I got to stay home and be a full-time mom but I wasn't really cut out for that so it came with many challenges. I thought it was a gift until I actually was doing it. I do feel that it was a gift for my kids, but a sacrifice for me. They got to have me all of the time and do things like swim in the ditch or climb a tree in their PJs. It was a gift that I had to learn *was* a gift. It would've been much easier to drop them off and pick them up after my work was done. I counted those minutes until bedtime every day. It's so hard being a stay-at-home mom. It's hard being a working mom. It's just hard being a mom. Not one is harder than the other; *it's just all hard.*

Motherhood is the one thing that will bring you to your knees, highlighting every self-doubt and negative thought you've ever had. It's like a flashing billboard you drive past on the highway that's flashing all of your baggage at you. I'm positive that I suffered from post-post-partum depression, but I just didn't reach out. The doctor actually wanted to hospitalize me for sleep deprivation, but unless they were going to allow both kids to come with me into the hospital that wasn't an option. There are days I look back and sometimes think I should've stuck with the "no kids" plan as I've messed up royally as a mom. I had once read that the children you are given are your mirrors; that they are your shadows. They're what you need to learn as your journey as a person to help you become the whole person you're meant to be. The last number of years of my life have really shown me that.

My marriage was not good. There were many more valleys than peaks and it kept getting harder. I felt completely isolated, on my own lonely island. Of course, I masked all of it so as to not let anyone see what was going on behind closed doors. I've never felt like my influence on my kids could ever outweigh the influence their dad had on them. I felt inferior and was trying my best, but it didn't matter how hard I tried, his influence was always louder than mine. I feel his voice is still louder than mine and he is deceased. It's like any influence I had would be wiped away by him, either intentionally or unintentionally. Sometimes I just think he didn't know any different. He was drowning in his own pain and trying to medicate himself to cope with that pain, but it was taking us all down with him. When you're in pain you want others to be in pain with you. It's more comfortable that way.

In May of 2010, I had just lost my step-dad to cancer and was going to the doctor for anti-depressants as my marriage was terrible. I was grieving, I had these young boys, and I was drowning. I know now I've battled depression my whole life. Without medication, I don't function well and it's not a great place to be. (*Take your little white pills if you need them - there's no shame in that.*) I had found a small lump in my breast the day before and because I'm A-type, I had drawn an x on the spot and asked the doctor to check it out since I was there anyway. I wasn't worried about it and really neither was the doctor but she decided to send me for diagnostics just to be safe. I never told anyone about it.

The day I went into the mammogram clinic I put my boys on the bus and headed into the city. There I was, age 34 with all of these older women waiting for their mammograms. They did it and then asked to do another one to get a different resolution. Prior to that, she had told me that the doctor would call me in 2-3 days with the results but after she did the scan she said I had to go immediately for an ultrasound. It went from "Your doctor will call you." to "On your way back stop at the clinic to see your doctor immediately."

Well fuck.

I remember pulling out onto the busy street from the diagnostic clinic. How I didn't get hit by oncoming traffic I don't know. I couldn't get my brain to work. It was swirling with fear and emotion, so I stopped and parked in a parking lot to collect my thoughts.

"It can't be that bad. God would not do this to me right now." I whispered to myself. We had just lost my grandpa to pancreatic cancer, my stepdad to lymphoma, and now me? There's no way this is real. I stopped in at the clinic on my way home and I could just feel the energy in the room when I walked in.

"It's bad Shannon."

"What do you mean it's bad? Bad like I'm going to die?" I said.

"You may or may not. I've tried to get ahold of your husband because I knew you'd be upset."

Like what the hell is going on here? Are you joking me? How can it be that bad? I just went for a mammogram a few hours ago. I needed to get home as my kids were getting off the bus and I had to take them to ball practice. She asked if I was ok to drive home by myself, but I didn't really have a choice.

I had wanted to find my husband to let him know, so I stopped in the field where he was on the way home. There were some men standing around having a beer, so I parked on the grid road and motioned for him to come over. He motioned for me to come over there to where he was and I was like, *no, you come here*, waving him over to me. I shared with him that I went to the doctor and was just told I had breast cancer. It didn't even clue in for him. He mumbled something about finding me a doctor and that was it. I drove away to go get the kids.

When I got home from the ball game he was drunk on the couch, passed out. He woke me up in the middle of the night and said, "Did you tell me you had breast cancer?" This was my journey; back to an even smaller island by myself, with sharks circling all around me.

Thankfully the diagnosis wasn't as grim as it was portrayed to me initially. The *you may or may not die* worked out in my favour. Secretly I thought that this diagnosis would help my husband see how important I was to him and the family, and he would finally see what he could potentially lose, and not want to lose it. That did not happen. The diagnosis just began a long process of much more dysfunction.

It's been eleven years since I was diagnosed with breast cancer. My sons were in Grade 2 and Grade 3 at the time. Treatment and healing was a long road with so many fears. I remember sitting in my son's room one night thinking, "If I do die, how am I going to leave my kids memories of me?" I had planned on buying them gifts for all of their milestones and having them put away somewhere so that they could be given to them at the appropriate time.

The fear that scared me the most though, was that I would be leaving them with their dad. I was terrified of that more than anything so I did not have a choice. Dying was not an option. My first goal was to live as long as I could to see them graduate and see them into adulthood. If God granted me that, I would be thankful. It would be enough for me. Of course, the longer I lived, I upped the ante a bit more but was careful not to get too greedy.

At the time of the diagnosis I was running marathons - literally running away from my life and all of the pain inside of the marriage. The running allowed me to centre my thoughts and my brain from the storm of everything else going on that no one knew about. I had just finished running a marathon at the end of May when I was diagnosed with cancer in June. I had felt perfectly fine and totally healthy. Mentally though, I was not healthy at all. I am a big believer that sometimes we need a kick in the ass and a slap in the face to really *get it*. I wouldn't wish cancer on my worst enemy but cancer was that kick in the ass for me.

I never wanted my kids to feel the way I felt as a kid; sharing parents, Christmases, and birthdays. I didn't want them to be the *divorced kids* in school. I was determined that was not going to be me. My *don't quit attitude* backfired on me. I had been told by one counsellor to pack my kids up in the middle of the night and leave my husband and I really wish I would've taken that advice. I didn't because I was terrified. I put on a great show that life was good but instead I isolated myself more and more as I protected the story, put up walls, and strategized what I would show people and what I wouldn't. I harboured guilt and shame toward myself because I knew better. I was raised better by powerful women.

The decision to finally leave was inspired by my grandmother. She was a strong woman, so strong that when she fell sick she lied to me about it so I wouldn't worry about her. When she was finally admitted to the hospital, I drove to go see her. The first thing she said when I walked into her room was, "What are you doing here?"feeling ashamed for me to see her like that. I spent the next week with her laying in a chair beside her bed as she was dying. I held her hand and played her fiddle music. As I reflected on the strength and resilience she had shown in her life, I had this thought of how disappointed she would be in me if I continued to stay in my marriage and allow my life to be this way. She would never have told me that to my face, but I just knew. After she passed, my grandfather told me that my grandmother had said, "I just don't know why Shannon is doing this? Why is she staying?"

I finally realized that in my quest and stubbornness to make sure my kids had a *good, normal life* I had somehow missed that they were already hurting so badly. We were all hurting. The dysfunction and trauma they experienced were something I held so much guilt for. I know that holding that guilt doesn't serve me or them, but as their mother, I just couldn't help but blame myself. I was starting to have some dark thoughts and thinking if I couldn't leave then I should just *leave*. Maybe it is me? Eventually, you start to believe the things that are told to you especially when you already have so many self-doubts swirling through your head.

The next step was figuring out how I was going to leave. How was I going to leave this beautiful farm and my horses? I didn't have a career as I was part of the family farm. I lived in a small town and you certainly can't let anyone know what's going on because word gets around and then I wouldn't be safe. My mom and I had to hatch a plan and I was very fortunate that my entire family rallied around me, and my grandfather gave me money for a down payment on a house.

It was devastating to tell my children as they were old enough to be able to make a stand if they didn't want to leave the farm. They had no idea what I was fighting for and they still don't know. It is my hope that one day they will be able to see that everything I did was for them. My goal as their mother is to support and love as much as I can so that any cycles of dysfunction and trauma do not continue as they grow older as men. I wanted finally for once in my life to feel safe in a place where I felt like I truly belonged and my kids and I were safe.

If people only knew what our life was like. It's embarrassing that a grown, educated woman who came from a line of solid, strong women, did this: made these choices. I know now that it all goes back to not feeling like I belonged when I was little, and there was a sense of security I felt with him. At the heart of who he was, my ex-husband was a great person. He had so many amazing characteristics but his demons were bigger than all of them while trying to portray his strength, his weaknesses took hold because he couldn't seek help. I thought I could love him enough to help him through it all. Turns out, I couldn't.

Your problems don't disappear just because you leave a toxic relationship. The damage and trauma was already done. I couldn't undo any of that. As the only parent left that my kids have, I take the anger and the pain. I'm the safe haven to receive it all because I'm going to love them unconditionally no matter what. I do know that those experiences made me who I am today and have allowed me to now help empower women to recognize their own worth long before I did.

I never allowed my kids to see me struggle and I believe that was a disservice to them. I tried to hide all of that pain from them. If I had to cry I would go into my bedroom closet, and lock the door to my bedroom or go into the shower. It may have been better for them to see my weakness at certain points in my life. Now, when they see some of that pain or I express my struggles it's very uncomfortable for them as grown men. I was always the safe place to land. I got all of the shit. I was the dump; the septic field for everyone's pain in the family.

As women, we need to find a healthy balance in life and for me, that comes through my horses. I love the smell of horses and if I could bottle up that scent and sell it I think I'd be rich. There is nothing like being with a horse especially when you're at your lowest. The outside of the horse is good for the inside of the soul. It's unexplainable until you feel it. You have to feel it. They take your emotional burdens from you and leave you with a lightness that is healing. If we take the time to be open and listen, horses have so much to teach us about ourselves. When I made the decision to leave my marriage I was also leaving my horses. Watching them drive out of the yard was so painful. I decided that my path with horses was done at that point and I wasn't meant to have them any longer so I shut the door on that chapter.

A few years later though a friend invited me to come to her arena and just ride. At first, I declined because I did not want to put myself in that vulnerable position of seeing those beautiful horses and knowing I could no longer have that for myself. It would be like ripping off a Band-Aid and pouring salt on a wound that was still open, but I did take her up on it and went. With my breast cancer surgery, I wasn't supposed to ride. Physically I was much weaker and I was insecure about my ability to ride again.

I was right back in the saddle, literally and figuratively. Shortly after, I had an opportunity to buy my heart horse, Ace. She is my accountability coach. She keeps my shit real. We have been on a journey together and we've both saved each other's life. I've helped figure her out and she's helped figure me out. I knew then I wanted to do more with horses and saw an opportunity to be an equine-assisted learning facilitator. I mulled it back and forth for almost an entire year and then one day I thought, "*Fuck it. I'm doing it.*" I knew I couldn't and shouldn't afford it, but I needed to get unstuck from wallowing in my grief and start moving forward and healing.

Two days into my certification program I had some serious doubts creep in and thought, "What the hell am I doing?" I had never been as mentally exhausted in my life as we moved through all of the course material. So often in life, we take the course, get the degree, certify in the program, and don't do anything with it. That wasn't going to be me though, I wanted to do something with this.

So I did. I followed my dream. Empower U Equine Learning Centre was formed to partner humans with horses for healing and growth. We bring people in from all different ages, abilities, backgrounds, and help them see the power that they have within themselves through the power of the horses. We just finished a 12-week objectively driven program of partnership of horses with women to empower them with key life skills and basic communication. We lose our way sometimes because we cannot communicate and problem-solve with others. The magic that happens with horses is indescribable. We are currently going through a program called "Power up to Read" which will help children with literacy skills in a completely different way with horses. This was a dream and a vision that I had but never thought could be a reality. It has become a real, very scary, sleepless night, but most amazing reality! I'm blessed to be partnered with my friend Barbie, who brings a totally different dynamic to our partnership and the two of us are unstoppable when we put our minds together.

My tenacity and *don't quit kind of attitude* has brought opportunities that I choose to see. When we choose to see opportunities and don't act on them, we are doing ourselves a disservice. How many women have dreams, hopes, and goals but don't act on them out of fear or self-doubt? I want to know that when I am on my deathbed, I can look back and say, "I didn't just think about it, I did it." I hope that I am showing other women that they can aspire to be all that they want to be and have everything they'd like for themselves and their families.

I have been blessed to be surrounded by very strong women in my life; resilient, courageous, caregivers. I look back at how scary it must've been for my mom after the divorce to move out on her own and forge her own way, moving back in with her parents and her siblings who were only 10 and 12 years old. My mom has always had a giving heart and a community mind. She always gave of herself and that has carried through into my life. She was never afraid to tackle a big project just because it was scary. Mom could wear many different hats: handy-man, taxi driver, cook and still worked full time. She managed everything with grace.

My step-mom never had children of her own and the two of us had a solid relationship. Not ever having her own children, I was all that she had. She was a school teacher, so had influenced many children over the course of her life. She was a strong influence in my life and my mom knew I would be safe with her when I was with my dad. She and my mom had a good relationship and appreciated one another. As a grown woman, I really appreciate the gift of that relationship between the two of them. We lost my step-mom to breast-cancer two years ago and I was honoured to sit with her and comfort her as she was dying from the disease that I had gone through just a few years before. I learned from both of them to never give up. It's just not an option to quit. You will figure it out. It's probably why I stuck around in my marriage much longer than I should've.

You cannot be an island and do everything on your own. There will always be challenges but figure out a plan and ask for help. Find your person: the one whom you can rely on when you need it most. If you're not safe, you need to be safe. I could've given up as there were times in my life when it seemed like the best option. I chose to live my best life through my adversity and trauma. Some days I do a better job than others but I'm always holding myself accountable. I'm always setting the bar higher for myself. Much too often we simply *grin and bear it* through motherhood. It does slowly eat away at us and affects so many other parts of our lives. Instead of grinning and bearing it, feel it and work through it to heal it.

Founded in 2018, EmPower U Equine partners humans with horses for success in developing skills for life, with the desire to help people become their most authentic self, while experiencing all that horses have to teach us. They offer Women's Empowerment Programs, Retreats & Workshops, Ladies Night Out & Date Night Events, Youth and Family Programs, Team Building Activities, Horse Camps, Riding Lessons, Equine First Aid, and so much more! EmPower U Equine serves the Northeastern Saskatchewan communities of Nipawin, Carrot River, Tisdale, Melfort, Aylsham, Prince Albert, & beyond! www.empoweruequine.ca

The Finish Line

The journey back to myself post-divorce really began the day I decided to lace up my running shoes and started training for a half-marathon. I can't recall what sparked the crazy idea. I had always loathed the idea of running, *literally loathed it.* I had zero experience and no training partner. It was just me, my shoes, my playlist, and an incredible amount of emotional turmoil to sort through.

I ran around the small town I lived in, day after day, piling kilometre after kilometre, and training to run 21 km. The outside noises were drowned out by the beat of my playlist, and I had nothing to do but leave it all out on the asphalt. *Mind over matter* was the mantra each time I wanted to quit. The matter for me was all the deep-seated grief, guilt, and fears that I could not solve with my conscious mind.

Running gave me two things: something to prove to myself (*hell yes, I can run 21 km - just watch me*) and an emotional release from my body that I so desperately needed. I got to experience the *runner's high*, something I had always heard about but never believed until I felt it myself. It's a euphoric feeling that is experienced via a release of endorphins by the brain. One foot in front of the other, heel to toe over and over again, I started on a journey to healing that cracked me wide open.

On the day of the run, the sun was warm and encouraging. It was a beautiful autumn day, the best weather you could ask for. I was there with a good friend of mine, Tracy, who was also running the half marathon that day. She had been a solid emotional support for me in the early months of the separation and we were running buddies that year. My kids were with their dad for the weekend, which made me quite sad as I so desperately wanted them there to see me cross the finish line. I wanted somebody there to celebrate the success of finishing the race, but the truth was I didn't need anybody at that finish line because this race was for me, only me, and not anybody else.

That last kilometre was like hitting a brick wall. It really took everything to keep trudging my heavy, weary legs forward and I don't think I could've done it without the race pace bunny, who happened to be my farm neighbour and an avid running enthusiast. I remember vividly that the tears started flowing as I saw the finish line and I could see a familiar face waiting for me at the finish line: my own mother. Of course, she was there, she'd never miss it. She never missed anything if she could help it. She was, and always will be, one of my biggest supporters. She brought my little nephews, who all had made big poster signs to welcome me across the finish line. I still treasure that photo of me with the boys and their signs to this day.

My goal was to run that half-marathon without stopping once and log a time of two hours and twenty minutes. I didn't stop once and I crossed the finish line in two hours and twelve minutes. The emotional marathon had already been run over and over in my head and would continue to replay over the years to come, but I did learn two lessons from those running days that have stuck with me to this day. First, we can do hard things and with the right mindset, we can do anything we want, period. Second, on hard days when you think you cannot get through another moment, the best thing to do is just put one foot in front of the other, and keep on going.

I found myself, over the years, crossing paths with and being inspired by other bold, confident and independent women who trudged through their hardships like a champ and made things happen for themselves and their loved ones, no matter what. One such woman was named Karen, the true definition of a single mother, whose son had been in my daughter's class since Kindergarten. I always admired how confident and bold she was and wondered how did she manage to do it all by herself? When I stared single motherhood in the face following the divorce, I was devastated and couldn't fathom how I could do it all on my own. I realized, I really wasn't going to be doing it all on my own. The kids still had a dad who was involved in their lives. Karen, on the other hand, always did it alone, and she raised one fine young man doing it.

As I listened to Karen share her story with me, I connected to so many parts of it. The ultra-independent woman who always finds a way, the problem solver, the fiercely loyal mother, they *tell me I can't and I'll prove you wrong* kind of woman. Karen is a pillar in her community. She is a healer, sharing her gifts to help others through their pain. I have immense respect for her and was honoured that she sat down with me to share a peek behind her closed doors. Her story of resilience, courage and grit is one that is shared by so many single mothers and I am grateful she chose to share it.

All on My Own

KAREN CAY

I've never been a person that needed other people. I'm incredibly self-reliant, which may be both a strength and a weakness. The truth is, I don't need anybody. I'm flexible because I've had to be. For me, things aren't black and white, but rather, grey. Plan A didn't work out for me so I moved on to plan B, then C, and I always have a plan D in the wings ready if I need it. Some people would say that's a trauma response, but I say it's part of a survival skill set. My creativity has always helped me to make something out of nothing and I'm proud to have taught my son that too.

I grew up in rural Saskatchewan on a farm with a brother who was five years younger than me. Mom always figured I had issues with him because she brought home this bouncy, beautiful boy from the hospital just in time for me to get kicked out to go to school. Five years is a considerable age difference and so we didn't have much in common. I should've had a sister, but my mother had a very late miscarriage in her pregnancy, which I think also affected our entire family dynamic.

Growing up on a farm, both mom and I were surrounded by men. I had an active role in helping out around the farm as I was the oldest child. I have always found it much more comfortable to be around men and I don't know if it's because I was raised around them, but I find working with men much easier than with women. I worked with many women, feminists ironically, who were the meanest, most competitive people on the face of the planet. Working with men was easier for me. They'd simply say, "Look you messed up, fix it." Which was easier to take than being stabbed in the back.

I didn't have many girlfriends in school. The community I grew up in was quite cliquey like most small-town schools. I had good friends but those friendships weren't super important to me. I went to school like I would a job. I didn't party or socialize much as I've always been a huge introvert. Our world was on our farm and my horse was everything.

I was a daddy's girl and my dad trained horses so that was something that we did together from the very beginning. I think a love of horses is something that isn't learned but is very much innate. If you're ever wondering about somebody introduce them to a horse. That horse will tell you everything you need to know.

Nichief, my horse, is incredibly wise. He is always with me energetically and is very much me. One time, I had to go fix his fence and it was incredibly windy, and horses hate wind. We got halfway across the field and I turned around to see my friend's son walking across the pasture. I was nervous for him as I sensed Nichief was unsettled. I too was agitated and annoyed, unreasonably mad. There was Nichief, standing at the top of the hill staring at me, shoulders up and on high alert. I was looking at him like, "Nichief, what is the matter with you!?" He just looked at me with that eye because horses can pick up a predator from 100 feet away and he was picking up on my rage and sensed a predator. That changed me forever. At that moment he showed me who I was. I was incredibly grateful for that lesson as I was trudging through some deep stuff in my life at that time. I needed that insight into myself that day and was grateful to Nichief for that.

From the time I was younger, I always assumed I would be a mom, but not a single mom. I got married to a man that not everyone approved of. That was hard, but I chose him over what others thought because I really wanted to have kids. We never were able to have kids though and, of course, when you can't have something, you really want it that much more.

I was with him for eleven years and then once we finally got married we broke up after eight months. I firmly believe that sometimes you need to get married to break up - it sounds crazy! Looking back, I knew we were done way before the marriage even happened, but it looked good on paper. It's what you do when you're both from good families in a small town. You settle down, you get married, and you have kids. That's what you do.

Our relationship was always unpredictable. In fact, it was awful. I don't know why I stayed except that I believed *I'm not a quitter*. The tower finally fell though. Actually, I pushed it over. He was cheating on me. I'll never forget the day he met me for lunch and I told him that I was going to go get my nose pierced. (I already knew he was cheating on me at this time). He said to me, "If you get your nose pierced, we're done." I said, "Really? Are you sure?", my voice dripped with sarcasm, as I knew he was sure, and I was sure too.

I drove home, packed up all of his shit and put it in my car to drive back to his mom's house. As I was driving my theme song from the Eagles, *I'm Already Gone* came on. I had this incredible serendipitous moment and a sense of joyful release. I just knew this was the right path for me. I went straight to get my nose pierced, headed over to the mall to get my photo taken in one of those instant photo booths, taped it on his shit, and threw it on his mom's lawn. That's it - done. In the lyrics, the song says, "How many times do we live our lives in chains and we never even know we have the key?" I let myself free.

I met my son's dad shortly after leaving my first husband - in fact, they were related. We got pregnant almost instantly after we got together which broke the myth from my first marriage that I was the one who couldn't have kids. I never thought that we would be a forever thing, but I hoped maybe he'd want to be part of his son's life.

At six months pregnant, I pulled up a carpet downstairs, and the next day started bleeding. I drove myself to the hospital and on the way, I would whisper to my sweet baby boy inside of me, "Are you ok?" and he would kick back at me. Once I got to the hospital, I filled out all of the forms, they checked me out and sent me home, but that mom survival instinct kicked in and I just knew things weren't ok. I decided to stay in the city, close to the hospital, and five minutes later I was sitting in the parking lot of the store when a gush of blood came out and there was blood everywhere. I drove myself back to the hospital, and standing in a pool of blood I was asked to fill out the forms again when the emergency doors burst open and they rushed me in.

Everything was a blur and I was sent home after a week's stay in the hospital. My mom came back to stay with me. The night I finally went into labour I was just seven months pregnant and I had an emergency C-section. Both of our lives were in jeopardy. I was at risk of bleeding to death and he was drowning in my blood. They got him out and the nurse said to me, "He's Ok." and they ran with him.

Even though I just had a C-section, I jumped off the gurney to go see him. Again, this was a mother's instinct. He was 3 pounds 2 oz., had no eyelashes or nails and they had to roll the preemie diaper three times to make it fit him. He was so tiny. They told me a few days later that they thought he had a fever. The doctor came in and said he didn't think he was going to make it as they thought he had meningitis. He had to have a spinal tap and I could hear his tiny screams from down the hallway. It was awful hearing those cries. I felt so helpless. For some reason though I knew he was going to be fine. He came through that fever and I was able to take my new baby boy home.

My son's dad went back to his former girlfriend shortly after the birth of our son but always kept coming back into our lives when it suited him. I remember laying on the floor one day, as we all do when we have nothing left in us. I had an 8-month-old baby that was 4.5 pounds. I had no help, no rest, and absolutely nothing left. I lay there and said aloud, "God, you have blessed me with this child, but you have to co-parent him with me now." I was a single mother and the sole breadwinner. There were so many moments when I questioned if I could keep doing it on my own, but I knew deep down that I could.

When Liam was almost two years old he started falling over. Prior to this, there were no signs of anything being wrong, so of course I immediately thought he had a brain tumour. The doctors ran all of these tests on him but still couldn't figure out what was wrong. Finally, they told me they thought the symptoms were manifesting as cerebral palsy. I sat there all by myself, with no one there to support me, no shoulder to lean on, and asked the doctor if it would get progressively worse. I had no clue how I was going to raise a son with cerebral palsy.

I drove home with him in the back in his little car seat and thought, "I'm by myself. This is terrible. How am I going to do this?" I knew I would have to just dig in; no excuses. He would be ok. I would be ok. It could be worse. All kids have something and this would be his *something*.

One day, my son's dad called and I decided I was just done. I had prayed and prayed about it, saying "God release me from this." I really think it was Spirit helping me. I had never taken a cent of child support from him but was ready to ask him for 11 years of backpay because I was just so done, and told him that. I told him that if he wanted to see our son I would accommodate that to which he replied, "Well, what's the point?"

"Well, it looks like we are done then." I said.

My son was eleven years old and I looked at him and told him that his dad was never coming back. I made sure Liam knew that his dad's issues were never about us. He never did come back, not once.

I've had to turn my pain into purpose so many times in life. When I was done with my maternity leave I had to think about how I was going to earn money and I knew I wasn't able to leave Liam to be raised by somebody else. I consciously chose a level of poverty to have a more abundant life with Liam. Part of it was my pride and the judgement I felt.

"You can't raise that kid alone." was what many people thought.

"Like hell I can't. I will, and I will do it while I stay at home and raise him too."

I landed a small reporter job for a local paper but it wasn't ideal so instead, I decided to start my own paper called *The Kinistino Clarion*. I bought a printer and did what I had to do to make it work. It was hard, but it was enough. Then, one day I got this phone call when I was really struggling. It was an answer to prayer again. I was offered an incredible job by another local paper, but I turned them down because I didn't want to move. The gentleman on the other side of the phone offering me this gig started to laugh and said, "Nobody turns me down." I simply told him it wasn't going to work for me and my son. I had my own thing going and I was surviving. He asked what they could do to get me on board and I suggested that I work from home as it was an online paper. Long story short, I got the job as a reporter for their community section and have been there for eleven years.

One of the most challenging things about being a single parent is that I had nobody that had my back. I had no backup, ever. I've always been really strict with Liam and acknowledge that perhaps we will be discussing this strictness in his therapy sessions ten years from now, but like my mom said to me, "You'll know when you're my age and you have your own kids."

Liam, for the most part, has been an easy kid to raise, other than his willpower, but I know he got that from his mama. If you want me to do something, try telling me I can't, same with my son. He's a leader, not a follower, which is what I wanted most for him to be. We are so lucky that during his time at school, he's never experienced any sort of systemic racism from any of the other students or friends since he is of Indigenous descent.

When Liam was little, some of the kids didn't want to play with him because he was too slow since he had a limp from cerebral palsy. As a mom, your first instinctive reaction is a defensive one, but instead, I challenged him to shift his perspective on it.

"It's not fair to ask them to slow down for you Liam. It's just not fair. Don't you want them to play their best too?." Instead, I started to send toy cars with him. I told him not to ask the other kids to play with him. Sure enough, they did ask him. Here's what I've learned in life: don't beg for attention or friendship. Don't chase anybody. My mom always used to say, "The second you're chasing, somebody's running."

I've made a lot of mistakes in my life but I've also learned from those mistakes. I learned that I am and always was somebody who would pick up people that needed fixing. That's what I was attracted to. That's why I attracted toxic relationships in my life. It's also why I chose to stay single for a long time after. Until I could trust that I was attracted to somebody who didn't need fixing, I wasn't going to introduce anyone into my son's life or my life. I had to fix myself first. I soon learned that I could still attract those people who needed fixing but instead I would make a business out of it.

I trained in Bowen therapy because it had worked for Liam; helping him with mobility. I had some extra money from a bonus I had received from my reporting job. The more I did it, the more I discovered I could do and feel other *stuff.* I was very much getting in touch with my intuitive side. One of my clients said something so profound to me one day. He told me not to be afraid of the gift I had been given and that really resonated. It pushed me to continue to be open and the more I did it the more I trusted myself. This was my first gift I realized. It has always been with me.

The only time I've ever gotten into trouble in my life is when I've strayed from my gut instinct. Why can't we just learn to trust our intuition, that voice inside, instead of having to learn the hard way? The hard times bring lessons and growth. You're going to look back at the hard times in your life with gratitude, but don't force the gratitude. Don't try to put roses on shit; that doesn't change what it is. Part of healing is regret and feeling stupid about the mistakes you made, but don't sit in that too long.

Motherhood has taught me so much. It's definitely messy. It's made me learn how to stick up for myself, and to demand respect instead of tolerating bullshit. Sometimes I can be a total bitch and sometimes my kid is an asshole and we have a bad day. Our kids learn by watching us. I want to make sure Liam understands that emotions are ok. He doesn't have to hold on to them or hide them.

The things you decide are important to teach your kids tell you who you really are. For me, lying is a deal breaker. We all stretch the truth and the lies that I've told have been the *presentation* lies. If you willfully deceive me though, we have a problem. We have nothing, if you're a liar.

Brutal honesty with other women is what's going to help set us free from behind these walls and masks of motherhood. There are blessings to be found in everything in our lives. At some point, you have to decide if you're a victim or a victor. Claiming victory doesn't deny the fact that shit happened in your life. Being a victor implies you once sat in victimhood. It means you have to continually work hard to keep your empire. There are always things or people trying to steal your empire. Some days we will let our masks down and let ourselves sit in the emotions and doubt but what's most important is that we learn for next time. There's always tomorrow. It always works out, because it has to.

Fitting In

Karen's words, "Brutal honesty with other women is what's going to help set us free from behind these walls and masks of motherhood." really hit me. So often we are anything but honest with one another about some of our deepest struggles and feelings about motherhood, marriage, or the true state of our mental health. It's not because we want to be dishonest or try to portray ourselves as something we are not. It's because the ball and chain of guilt that we carry is heavy. There's this crazy collective expectation that we are supposed to love every minute of motherhood and marriage, without question.

Each edition of the *Strong as Mother* series brought new topics and new feelings to the surface with each new panel of women and audience who held space for them. We spoke about things openly that often get filed in the *do not touch drawer* of motherhood. The tears and laughter formed a common connected bond between those who attended, and I always left the evening feeling lighter and more connected to not only other women but also myself. Feeling these connections are two things that had felt like I had been missing often in my life.

I struggled to fit in when I was a teen and often felt like I was just never enough. I was the captain of the high school volleyball team, the

SRC president, and the editor of not one, but three yearbooks yet still, I felt like I had more to prove. As a high-achieving student with pretty solid marks, I remember still the disappointment I had with myself about not getting more academic awards in our Grade 12 year despite having a 92% average. Looking back now, I realize I had this *never-enough* mindset that kept me seeking to achieve more and pleasing those around me, which continued throughout my adulthood and still lingers today.

As a people pleaser, you can easily *spot* other people pleasers. We have many of the same traits and characteristics. We will be the first to offer a helping hand and the last to leave until everything is cleaned up or put away. We will rarely say no, even if it means sacrificing sacred time away from our own loved ones. We have a hard time setting emotional boundaries and we are determined to fix any and all problems that come our way, feeling unsettled until we can help make something better. We feel emotions in big ways, and we often can be misunderstood or judged.

I knew I had met a fellow people pleaser when I met Cassie. She's a dynamite, go-getter, no holds back, fire-cracker kind of woman. Her appearance on the *Strong as a Mother* panel is one I won't forget, as she spoke candidly about what it's like to try and fit in somewhere you don't feel like you really belong. Not only did she experience divorce as a child but also adoption. As I sat with her and listened to her share her story for this book, we shared some tears, some laughter, and a common bond of two women who knew divorce well, and who knew what it felt like to not fit in, but from different perspectives. Cassie is strong, outspoken, and never afraid to show who she really is. She has turned her pain into purpose in more than one way and loves those closest to her deeply.

Build Your Own Family

CASSIE DAVIS

From the time I was very young, I always knew that I was adopted. I don't have a tragic story or memory of the day I found out. I actually don't even remember it all as I was three months old when I was adopted. The way the adoption laws worked back in the 1980s was that a biological family had three months to change their minds about adoption, so my adoptive parents decided to leave me in foster care until my biological parents' rights ran out. Two days before Christmas they got the phone call, all rights had passed, and they were able to have me.

Biologically, I'm the oldest child, but adoptive-wise, I'm the youngest. My adopted brother and I are six years apart as our family adopted him before me, but we look so much alike kids in school often thought we were biologically related.

As a young girl, I loved dance, ball, and poetry. I was confident and played with everyone. I had a huge heart for special needs children as my adoptive father was 75% deaf. Life changed when I was six years old when my adoptive dad left us. My brother was twelve years old and so he stepped into taking on the *dad* role for us which he took very seriously.

Mom raised us as a single mother our entire childhood. She never dated or re-married and gave everything to make sure we could be in dance and gymnastics while working her job to provide for us. Looking back I absolutely recognize the sacrifices Mom made for us as she never had time or money for herself. My brother trained six days a week, six hours a day as a competitive gymnast so I rarely saw him, but he was a great brother. He always stepped in when I needed and taught me the things that I needed to know.

I'm an emotional person who grew up with an adoptive mother who wasn't raised to be emotional. It was difficult not to have my emotional needs met as a child, but I couldn't ask her to be someone she wasn't. I was very lucky to have a neighbour, Diane, whom I loved like a mother. She was the emotional support that I longed for in my own mother who wasn't comfortable with the touchy-feely stuff. Diane had a son and she would bake cookies with us and do stained glass Gingerbread houses every year with us; those traditions were very important to me. Every time I did well in school and shared it with her she'd say, "I knew you could!" and was thrilled and so proud of me. We would have movie nights and I would play with her hair until she fell asleep. Her house felt like home.

I can't imagine what life as a child would've been like without Diane. So many things I do now as a parent with my own kids are all because of her: things like Christmas traditions, gift wrapping, and cookie baking being some of them. My mother couldn't have afforded to do those things with us and it definitely wasn't who she was. In Grade 10, I wrote a poem called *1201* which was our house address. I wrote about going to 1136 which was Diane's house, where everything was quiet and calm, and felt so much like *family*, but then I would have to go back to 1201. That hit my mom hard, but it was really how I felt.

Part of being an adoptee is a strong desire to have others like and accept you. We do anything to make people like us, even if we know that it's not who we are. Anytime I was put in a group project in school I would always do all of it; so everyone liked me. I needed to be liked so badly I would go the extra mile for it. I've always been a people pleaser.

One of the most profound moments of my life was when our big family tree was brought out at a family event. I saw all the names written on the tree and then saw the word *adopted* beside my name. I had to will myself not to cry and let everyone see how much it upset me. It was blatant. I didn't truly belong in that family. I'm here, and they'll put my name on the tree, but it's necessary to make sure everyone knows that I'm adopted. I thought to myself, "I am a dead branch." That experience was so impactful to me that it prompted me to write about being a *bracke*t and never feeling like I truly belonged in my adoptive family no matter how hard they tried to make me feel loved and accepted.

All the TV shows when we were younger were all family shows, including Full House, Family Matters, and The Fresh Prince of Bel Air. I always just thought "That's my biological family - that's what they're going to be like."

I went back and forth in my mind about the decision to meet my biological parents. The adoption records are bullshit really. You get very little updated information and Saskatchewan has some of the worst adoption laws. We don't get the right as adoptees to get updated medical history on our biological family. In other provinces, I could've just filed a form saying I needed access to that medical history and my biological family would have to update my records for me. That's not the case in Saskatchewan. Not all of us want to meet our biological family, we just want to know if breast cancer runs in the family. If I need a kidney, I need to know who may be a match.

I always thought that meeting my biological parents would feel like coming home. I would run to them and they'd gather me up in their arms, they would have a party for me with gifts waiting, but it was nothing like that. My adoptive brother warned me that before starting the process of finding them that it was important to have one's *shit* in order. I never really knew what he meant by that, until I did.

I was 24 when I met them and my biological mother couldn't even look me in the eye. I had brought all of these pictures from my childhood for her to look at, thinking surely she'd want to see them. She looked at them but didn't look up at me once, nor did she speak. My biological dad on the other hand was super pumped to meet me, but that was all a little too much for me. He was calling himself *dad* and it felt awkward. I have a dad already, but thanks.

No one even knew my mother was pregnant with me. To everyone else, I was a hidden secret. My biological grandmother was the only other family member who knew I existed from the beginning. The nurses told my mother that it would be easiest if she never held me so I was never held. I was brought straight to the nursery. My grandmother worked at the hospital and had heard from a nurse that my mother and father were placing me up for adoption. She came upstairs just as I was being taken to social services and she was allowed to hold me. She was the only one that ever held me.

My parents didn't discover they were even pregnant with me until my mother was seven months pregnant and then she delivered me at eight months. They were due to get married in October and had me in September. They had me, got rid of me (or placed me so to speak), got married, and never spoke of it ever again. She eventually did tell one of my uncles about me since she cried often.

I was told that my biological parents placed me because they just didn't feel financially ready to take on a child. They were 19 and 21 years old. I feel like they could've stepped up but they felt they wanted more for me, so gave me up. It's hard for me because I feel they could've done it. It would've been hard, but they could've done it. They got married just after placing me up for adoption and then had a son. I have a biological brother who is 18 months younger than me. He did not know I existed until he was 14 years old. He thought he was an only child. He was told never to speak about it again. Ever since I was very small I would dream about my biological brother. In my dreams his name was Matthew, but his name is actually Steven. In the dream, we would be at my birthday party. I always knew that I had a biological brother, so when I found out about him I was not surprised.

Everyone always says that adoption is about giving the child a better life, but then they put you somewhere that you don't really belong and as an adoptee, that's hard. You never know where you fit, ever. You become someone else's child and their dream in their family. Often people adopt because they can't have their own children, so I felt like I was a *Plan B* even to begin with. My family would've had their own children if they could. I felt like I was never someone's first choice.

It's difficult to speak up about your own trauma and feelings as an adoptee since you want to try and be grateful for the life you have. If ever you sound ungrateful you hear, "Well they kept you. They could've aborted you." The opposite of adoption is not abortion, it's parenting. In my situation, my biological mother had decided to carry me until I was born. She was seven months pregnant when she found out she was pregnant with me so abortion wasn't on the table, however, she could've kept me.

I only saw my biological mother once after that first meeting and have never spoken to her again. The adoption worker had noted in my adoption papers that my mother had the most abnormal emotional wall built up that she had ever seen, indicating that there was a sense of relief on my mother's part when she signed the papers. Her perception was that my mother was very detached from the whole experience of having me. I think that's just how she coped, to detach from me. I imagine that I am very triggering for her. There is very little support given to biological parents after placing a child up for adoption now and there was even less then. My brother said that once they told him about me, our parents would fight constantly, pointing fingers at one another. When Steve was 18, our biological parents divorced.

Both my adoptive and biological fathers came in and out of my life until I finally set emotional boundaries. The back and forth wasn't healthy for me. Either you're in or you're out. My biological father decided not to be part of my life after I laid it on the line for him. His emotional dysregulation and toxic behaviours were so unhealthy that they trickled down and affected my relationship with Steve, my biological brother. Steve eventually saw our father's true colors and we were able to continue having a relationship.

When I got pregnant I experienced this huge feeling of relief that I could have biological kids that would actually be *mine*. Carson, my first child, was the first person I was genetically related to that I could acknowledge and be acknowledged by. He was my *real* son and I was his *real* mom. I've always been protective of my two kids. I hover, yes I definitely hover. It's important to me to build everything I can with them from memories to traditions and let them be whomever they want to be, chasing their own passions. I want them to know that they are not defined by their family. They can be whom they want to be.

Life often throws us curve balls when we least expect it and I got a big one at the age of 33 when I was diagnosed with cervical cancer. I wasn't due for a regular pap test, but my doctor was going on maternity leave so she was swabbing everybody before she left. The report indicated that I had cells which likely could become cervical cancer. I went in to meet with my OBGYN who seemed not to be worried at all about it at first. She took the biopsy and I went in for a leep procedure. That's when things began to go wrong and I almost needed a blood transfusion. They found the second cancer which is what was causing the bleeding during the procedure. It was stage zero but she told me that if she didn't get it out of me now, I might not see Christmas. The doctor said that once this type of Cancer hits stage two there's really nothing they can do. I got the call for the date for my surgery when I was driving home from that appointment. That's how urgent it was. Twenty-eight days later, I had a full hysterectomy. They took everything but my ovaries.

While I waited for the surgery I was in a constant state of fear, thinking it had already grown, and that I would have to start planning for my funeral. I started journaling to the kids every day, writing down memories I had of them. I immediately was fearful I wouldn't be there for my daughter's wedding, just like my biological mother wasn't there for my own.

It was so shocking to hear, I wasn't really prepared for it. I got really lucky. It was a dark time, but I got through it. After that, I decided to stop living for other people. I had always been a people pleaser. At the time I was not in a fulfilling career. At the end of the day, we spend way too much time at work to be doing something that we aren't fully passionate about. Part of me wondered what had I been saved for? I'm here for a reason. What do I do now?

I always have been passionate about helping people, volunteering, and doing charity work. People with addictions always had my heart. It's trauma that causes addiction; not the drug, alcohol, or substance.

The substance is the temporary solution to the trauma and no one wants to talk about the trauma. I wanted to start helping others to talk about their trauma, to realize that they can be so much more than what happened to them, so I decided to become a licensed therapist with a specialty in addictions. I also wanted to work with adoptees.

I am most proud of deciding to finally go after it, my dream. My husband and I just sold a franchise that we bought at the age of 27. I think people thought that we were completely crazy. It wasn't happiness for us. Finally, we are living our true happiness, moving out to the farm and living the life we want to live. I know this is where I'm supposed to be and things are aligning perfectly for it all to happen.

For any women or mothers reading this who are adoptees and struggling with their identity or trying to make sense of things my advice to you is this; *build your own.* Build whatever feels authentic to you, whether it be traditions or traits from your biological family or adoptive family, and go with whatever feels most natural for you instead of trying to please other people. Finding your own truth is imperative to growing.

Cassie Davis is a registered practicing counsellor in Melfort, Saskatchewan. She works with adoptees to process their trauma, working through attachment issues, guilt, grief, sense of self and loss in a supportive environment. If you are an adoptee, biological parent or adoptive parent, Cassie is trained to help guide you in the process of healing.

Website: www.simplybecounselling.ca
Email: cassie@simplybecounselling.ca

Helpless

There are some things that happen in the world that are so impactful on our lives that we will never forget where we were and what we were doing when the news broke. There are three that stand out in my mind. The day Princess Diana died in 1997, the attacks on the twin towers in 2001, and the Humboldt Broncos bus accident in 2018. I can literally paint a picture in my mind of exactly what I was doing at the time of each of those horrific events. The day I heard the news of the Broncos accident, it first came to me via a text from my daughter. Like every other mother listening and watching nationwide, the grief in my heart felt crushing every time I read that another death had been confirmed. I felt incredibly helpless and so heavy with sadness. Our province of Saskatchewan and the entire nation had just been reminded of the sobering, stark reality that our lives can literally change in an instant. The collective shadow of grief still hovers over our province to this day and I hold all of those sweet mamas and families who lost their beloved boys that day so close to my heart.

In March of 2019, my husband and I were co-hosting a *Mindfulness for Couples* evening at a local restaurant. There were couples we knew who attended and many couples who were new faces to us. One couple was sitting close to the front of where Alan and I were speaking. I had never met them before but I remember the husband, Chris, speaking up on a few topics that we were addressing. I didn't know who he was, but thought he definitely had deep insight and understanding of mindfulness and conscious living practices. For a man, he sure spoke openly and confidently about mental health.

Later on that night my sister, who was in attendance also, whispered to me, "Do you know that couple sitting over there? That's Chris Beaudry. He was the assistant coach of the Humboldt Broncos and the only one from the team who was not on the bus at the time of the Bronco's bus accident." she said.

Oh, THAT'S Chris Beaudry, I thought to myself. *That's why he was so insightful when we spoke of mental health and mindfulness.* I instantly felt that heavy grey cloud of sadness and empathy in my heart imagining what he must've gone through in the trauma of losing seventeen team members and friends. I later found out that he had seen the advertising for the couple's event I was hosting on a virtual platform and on a whim, booked tickets for him and his wife, Richelle. I hadn't had the opportunity to speak much with his wife that night, but later on developed a lasting friendship with her.

Chris and I connected after the event and we ended up doing some youth mental health speaking engagements and events together. His raw, honesty in sharing his story of pain, addiction, grief, and recovery makes him so relatable. He develops this trust connecting with others through being vulnerable himself and opens a door to healing and hope for others who've experienced trauma, addiction, and loss. By giving himself permission to be vulnerable and share his story, he gives others permission to do the same without fear or regret. I am grateful for the day Chris and Richelle showed up at our event. I've learned so much from him since then. He's helped me challenge some of my own limiting belief systems and fears and has helped me sift and sort through some painful layers of my own.

Behind the scenes in Chris' recovery and healing was this beautiful, strong soul I had the opportunity to become friends with, his wife, Richelle. I had invited her to be a guest on one of the virtual editions of my *Strong as a Mother* series during the pandemic to speak about the supportive role she had in regards to the trauma and healing her husband experienced. In hearing her share her story, I was reminded that stories always have layers. Richelle, became the anchor and safe haven during a time of immense grief and trauma, and like so many wives and mothers, it came at the expense of her own emotional needs. Richelle has this grounding, nurturing energy to her and a wisdom that feels like her soul has walked many journeys. She is an exceptional and intuitive mother who is deeply connected to nature and animals; she's always loving on everything and everyone! Richelle loves with her whole heart and in sharing her story, offers a unique perspective on what it's like to love unconditionally.

Finding My Own Way

RICHELLE BEAUDRY

I was born an only child and raised by both a single mother and my grandmother. Looking back now, I can see where some of my trauma came from as I was either on my own or only with adults all of the time. My mom was 21 when she had me and tried living on her own for a bit. After three months, she had to go back to work, so we moved in with my grandmother. We lived with her until I graduated. My mother lived with my grandmother until she was put in a senior's facility.

I've always wanted to be a mother. As a child, I babysat from the time I could; usually multiple families at a time. I was the one kid that chose to babysit over partying.

I didn't really have a relationship with my father. He never told his parents about me when my mom became pregnant. It's just been recently that I started talking to him more. I've recently come to learn some of the trauma he experienced, so I have a bit of a softer spot for him now.

I married Chris when we were 22 years old, and we actually started trying to have kids before we were even married. Nothing was coming of it and we didn't really think too much about it. We tried and tried and six years in we realized we would need some help so we went to a fertility clinic. We both got tested and found out that it was him that was preventing us from getting pregnant, not me. We did IUI thirteen times with his sperm and nothing took. Nine years into our journey we decided we would try with a donor. We were given the donor site and both picked the same one. We received four donor specimens to use and the first two didn't take. After the third try, we decided to go away on a holiday. When we got back we found out that we were pregnant, a huge triumph for us!

We both assumed that the donor sperm had worked. Nine months went by and when our first daughter, Emily, was born, as soon as she came out I looked at her and exclaimed, "You look like your dad!" Chris replied, "Don't do that Richelle. Don't do that." I just knew that she looked so much like Chris. There was a chance that he was the biological father because each time we had gone through the donor process we had tried to conceive on that very same day, just in case.

It took us a few months before we got the courage to get a DNA test done on Emily to determine if she was in fact Chris' baby. When she was four months old, we had the test done. We got the results back and they were 99.999% positive that Emily was Chris's child.

We talked about what changed from us not being able to conceive for nine years to then, unexpectedly, being able to conceive Emily. We've since discovered that the clinic we used didn't have a great reputation in Canada; one of the worst actually. They didn't guide or require us to make any dietary or lifestyle changes throughout the process. It felt like they just took our money and we were left to put all of our hopes and dreams in the process. Looking back, we got pregnant because Chris had made the conscious choice to quit drinking. Prior to that, he had an alcohol and prescription drug addiction. He had been in a few major accidents where he had sustained injuries and was overprescribed oxycontin. Chris had stopped drinking and we were making better, more conscious lifestyle choices when it came to diet and behaviors. When we got pregnant with our second child, Sophie, we were successful the first month we tried.

I really didn't allow myself to be a mother fully at first. I felt that as a farm wife, I had to keep myself busy. I wasn't bringing home the bucks, so I had to make sure that I was always doing something at home. Chris was gone on the road coaching hockey quite a bit, so I was a busy mom at home with two little ones. I didn't take the time to cuddle at bedtime or be present with them when I knew I should've been. It was hard on our marriage because I wanted to fully enjoy motherhood, but felt like I always had jobs and duties I had to complete. We also differed in some of our beliefs about parenting. I was not the *let them cry it out* kind of parent, and he was at that time, so there was often conflict when it came to those sorts of things.

A week or two before the Bronco bus accident, we found out that we were pregnant with our third child, Lily. The morning of the accident we were in Regina at a hockey event and I was experiencing some bleeding. I was planning on going to the doctor when we got home if the bleeding didn't stop. Chris had been with the Broncos hockey team for a few years, doing analytics at first and then he became the assistant coach during the year of the accident. He had known many of the players from previous hockey programs. On the day of the accident, he was the only one who was not on the bus, yet he was supposed to be on it. He had messaged the other assistant coach, Mark Cross, that day and said that he was going to try and hop on the bus at Tisdale with the rest of the team. That afternoon when we got back from Regina, he had laid down for a nap. I was supposed to wake him up, but knew he was exhausted and could use a bit longer of a nap before the game. The only reason he wasn't on that bus is because I didn't wake him up from his nap, and he had to drive on his own. Had he been on the bus with the team, he would've died. His seat was right up at the front by the other coaches, Mark and Darcy, who both died that day. There's no doubt that Chris would've died that day had be been on that bus.

Chris was about 20 minutes behind the bus and came upon the accident. He called me and said, "There's been an accident and it's really bad. I think you should go to your mom's house." My initial thought was, *I'm sure it's not that bad. I'm just going to stay home and do what I can from here.* He called my mom and asked her to come stay with me and the girls. I thought when Chris said it was *bad* that it meant likely a few deaths. Five deaths would be really bad, I thought. I had no idea how bad it really was until later. He called me to check in a few times and I had called his aunt to go be with him since I knew he wouldn't be able to drive home himself. My phone kept ringing as people were trying to get updates and news about their loved ones. He got home about midnight and then got a call around 3:00 am to go into the morgue.

Because Chris was the only one able to, he was called to the morgue to identify all of the bodies of the players. Many of the player's parents didn't even know he had done that until he gave his impact statement in court. That process in itself is an unimaginable trauma for one person to experience.

I didn't lose a husband that day, but I *lost* my husband. Chris was *gone*: mentally, physically, and emotionally. He was gone for the next six months and not able to be fully present or connected. He was never the same again. He was physically there, sometimes emotionally there, but he was always one trigger away from slipping back into the bathtub to have his own time to grieve. I had to figure out how to give him the space he needed to heal, but I also had to figure out how to continue to parent the girls while supporting Chris through it all. I put myself on the back burner for the next year and a half. I felt I wasn't as needed, so I did start to get very sad. He changed so many times throughout his healing journey and then began his spiritual journey. It was challenging, as I felt like he dove straight in from grieving to his spiritual practice and it was hard to know what my role was at that point, so I mostly just focused on being a mom.

He was three years sober prior to the Broncos bus accident and although I was fairly confident he wouldn't slip back into his previous addictions, there were times that I worried. I know how strong-minded he is but that is an incredible amount of trauma to process and he did almost slip a few months later. He had called me crying one night when he was away. He wanted to just numb it all. It was definitely challenging growing a baby throughout that entire time, especially when he wasn't able to be fully present for us. I don't think Chris came to any pre-natal appointments with me. I had to hold so much of it all emotionally on my own.

I feel like I've married and buried seven different versions of Chris in the two years following the Broncos accident. I can tell he's having a bad day by the songs he's listening to. I didn't even grieve the loss of the *old* Chris until we attended a funeral of a good friend of ours that was killed in a snowmobile accident. His funeral broke me open and brought all the grief I had been stuffing. I cried for days and days. The year after that, we had a puppy that died in front of us and that brought on the rest of the grief that was lying dormant. I cried for two weeks. It had all re-surfaced as it finally felt safe to process my own grief.

After our third child was born, and almost a year to the day of the Bronco accident, Chris found out his mom was diagnosed with pancreatic cancer. Lily was a baby, just seven months old, when Chris's mother died. She was in the room when Bev died and we all just knew that Lily could sense and feel Bev's spirit leaving her body. Chris had experienced absolutely unimaginable loss in the span of one year; so much grief.

I did feel a bit resentful at times as a wife when Chris was exploring new experiences in his healing journey. He was going off to retreats and I was left behind to parent our girls. I do know that it was a necessary part of his journey and I was and always will be, fully supportive. I was just exhausted from everything. Being a part of Chris' healing journey as his wife taught me ultimate compassion and what it feels like to provide safe energy for someone processing an immense amount of grief.

I'm now finding my own ways to grow. I've recently started exploring somatic experiences and found a mentor. I've been drawn to homesteading and have been focusing on healthy lifestyles for my family. I've started a little market in my community and bring in healthy products to share with others. We just took a huge leap and bought a rural property that has its' own little lake; 19.5 acres with a small house. We aren't moving yet but we are excited for what may be ahead for us and it feels good to finally make decisions for us, as a unit. We always talked about owning a property in the forest, with water and now we do.

Our three daughters, as a result of our own experiences of trauma and grief, have also experienced it and undoubtedly, it's affected them as well. Our oldest Emily, is an empath, she can feel the energies in the room and she takes them on. Sophie is 100% authentic and someone everyone should be like. She truly lives her life as who she is. Lily is a light. Her energy is so strong. She's so damn happy and loves everyone. For everything she was through emotionally as a baby and child, she really is just light and love.

Motherhood has given me the opportunity to experience a love I would have truly never imagined. It makes me feel overwhelmed and angry, so quickly and intensely. Then it's gone and I feel immense blessings again. I am most proud of myself for sticking through it all: through the hard times of supporting my husband while he healed from addictions and the immense grief he experienced. It pushed me to be a more mindful, gentler mother. It would've been easier to run away but I didn't. I am proud of myself for that.

Through the Lens of a Child

The older I get as a parent the more I realize how special the time at bedtime is with my children. Regretfully, when my two older children were little, I was much too *busy* and overwhelmed to lay with them for more than a few minutes at bedtime. That's time you don't get back, and I really do regret it. Now, as my oldest finishes off Grade 12 and my littlest is about to enter into Kindergarten, I make much more of an effort to connect with all four kids at bedtime since that's when the magical conversations happen.

One night at bedtime, I asked my 8-year-old son, Hudson, what he would be if he could be anything in the world, and not fail at it. His answer caught me off guard but was just what I needed to hear. He said simply, "I'd be a kid".

I thought for a moment, out of all of the things he could be, why would he say that? Then it hit me! Of course, he said that, because kids live in the moment. They aren't looking ahead wishfully to the next thing or lamenting about the past. They are living literally *and joyfully* in the moment.

He followed that by saying, "I'll always be a kid , Mom. Even when I'm a grandpa, I'll still be your kid and I'll never, ever forget you." (Cue the big alligator mom tears.)

There's so much extra to process in our lives these days it seems since the start of the pandemic, and so many things we can choose to stress about, fixate on, or worry about. That night, I choose to really soak up those magical few minutes lying in bed and being reminded by my introspective little boy to live joyfully in the moment.

Hudson is our child who requires a bit more energy (and patience) when it comes to parenting. He has a very active imagination that interrupts his sleep and a busy brain that challenges his ability to focus which sometimes gets him into trouble. He also has the tendency to fixate on things. He is a bright student, who excels at reading and math and understands the workings of his own brain. One day, he came home from school and said, "Mom, sometimes it's hard for me focus and I get off track." We talked about the mindfulness and breathing strategies we've learned and how he can self-regulate to get himself back on track when he needs.

Hudson also feels emotions in big ways. He is sensitive and cries easily. In fact, he was the sole inspiration behind my second children's book, "Elliot's Rainbow Rollercoaster", a book about big emotions. We talk openly about emotions in our home and try our best to create a safe space for that. Him and his dad were in a bit of a power struggle one day that resulted in tears for Hudson. My husband told him, "That's enough crying." as many of us would say. Hudson's response was, "Dad, you can't tell people when they've had enough of crying. If I'm sad, I'm sad." *Yes!* - that's the way I want my children to feel. If your expression of your emotions make someone else feel uncomfortable, that's not your issue, it's theirs. Hiding our emotions doesn't make them go away.

Hudson has a brilliant creative side. He loves music and has been able to catch any beat since he was six months old. One of my favourite videos of him is from when he was just a baby playing the drums with my husband and was surprisingly spot on the beat. He has the softest, squishiest heart that allows him to love and connect to others in very sensitive ways, yet, he may struggle with some things in life because his brain works differently than others. We talk about these unique gifts as *superpowers;* like Lily, the character in my first children's book, *Lily's Loud Mout*h. She has the superpower of having a *loud mouth* and using her voice to stand up for what she believes in. Feeling emotions in big ways can be a superpower too - we just have to learn how to make that superpower work best for us.

Since the dawn of time, kids have been born into this world that don't necessarily fit "inside the box". Kids who challenge belief systems about what a *good kid* is and what a *good kid* does. That doesn't make them *bad kids*. Often they are misunderstood and misjudged. They struggle, and find coping mechanisms along the way. Some are healthy coping mechanisms and some are not. As mothers, we need to allow them to learn and grow, but be there for guidance when they make mistakes.

One of the mothers that I was blessed to meet on the *Strong as a Mother* journey was born during an era when kids were expected to be seen, and not heard. There were strict expectations about how kids were to behave and not much empathy or understanding for kids whose brains weren't wired like that. Carman learned many lessons that helped mould her on her own journey through motherhood and grandmotherhood. Sitting with her for this interview I felt like I was speaking to a version of my own grandmother, and I am proud to call Carman my friend and admire the love and devotion she has for her family. Carman is genuine and her words are always straight and to the point. She has wisdom and grounding energy that feels very warm and welcoming, and I feel so thankful our paths crossed.

Wild Child

CARMAN NYGAARD

I was a wild child; untamed, stubborn and way too energetic for my family. I was like Tigger from Winnie the Pooh, bouncing around all of the time. I was always too much for everyone. I remember my grandfather taking me in the old grain truck one day when I was little and he ended up turning around to take me back to be with Grandma because I was bouncing in the seat with all of this energy that was just too much for him. Back in those days, you were to be seen and not heard as a child.

At the age of 7, I was diagnosed with ADHD. Dad was so angry with mom for taking me to the clinic to get that diagnosis, because in those days, people didn't air their affairs in public. The doctors wanted to medicate me but my mother wouldn't let them.

I remember being disciplined when I was *bad* and getting locked in my room and tearing my curtains down. I ripped all of the wall-paper off of my walls or flipped my bed over. I wasn't trying to get even with my parents but I just couldn't control myself or my emotions. My mother tried so hard with me, spending hours playing with me outside or cutting out paper dolls from the Sears catalogue to keep me focused and busy. I was definitely a child that required work.

Mom had four children in five years and got tired out from all of us very easily. She had a heavy hand and did 99% of the discipline. Dad wasn't really part of the parenting process as he was always in the field. The truth is dad never had any tools to deal with us. He wasn't raised to raise kids. Mentally he would shut us out and just go to the field to work, so mom was left to deal with it all. He certainly wasn't a poor father, but he didn't have the tools.

At the age of 36, my mom had a hysterectomy, followed by a full-blown nervous breakdown that year as well. She tried to take her life and wound up in the hospital for quite some time. Back then, men rarely recognized their wives needed rest and that they needed help. My grandfather was a German war vet and very hard and callous. You could see the steel in his eyes. My father was the youngest of two boys in his family, so he struggled with his own father. His mental health suffered because of it and it spilled over to his marriage as well. My dad did get my mom *house help* after her breakdown.

As the oldest girl, I was always the *adult* in the family. My mother was an alcoholic from the time I was little. It wasn't really the amount she drank, but rather what the booze did to her that mattered most. My parents split when I was 13 years old and the first time mom quit drinking was when I was 14 years old.

I was my mother's keeper during her journey to sobriety. My job was to cook meals and bring them out to the field and take care of whatever was necessary for our family. Mom's mental health challenges continued as her life turned into a whirlwind after she and Dad divorced.

After mom and dad split, we moved away to Manitoba and lived there for eleven months. In that time Dad never called us. I don't ever remember him calling any of us, not once. It affected my younger sister. I remember feeling so sad for her. I seemed to be able to handle it much better than her. Dad struggled with expressing his emotions and I don't ever remember him telling us that he loved us. He had love, understanding, and patience which I didn't see until much later on in life. At the time, we very much felt emotionally abandoned by him. He turned out to be the best grandfather any child could ask for, teaching the kids about hunting and the history of Saskatchewan through his love for the museum. He was a great and kind man and holds a very large piece of our hearts.

My step-father became an important role model in my life and he taught me what love was. He and I had a very solid connection that I am still grateful for to this day. My brothers might see him in a different light, but I can say that he really showed me what a bond between a daughter and a father could be. He and my mom ended up separating later on in their relationship because he was having an affair with someone online which triggered my mother's mental health issues again in the face of rejection.

My mother and sister have struggled throughout their lives with anxiety, depression, and mental health challenges. As I grew older, and had my own family, it's been incredibly hard to support them from afar. When my mom is sick, my sister is sick, and vice versa. My sister is my hero. She can bounce back from all the challenges she's faced. After she tried to take her own life, I remember feeling so angry with her. I thought to myself, "How dare you try to take yourself away from all of us? You're as much a part of me as my own children and I need you in my life." That was a real eye-opener for me to realize that I needed her so much. It was also hard for me to realize that at age 58 I still needed my mother as much as I needed her when I was a child.

I've always been caring for people and deep down inside I think I was just programmed that way. It's who I've always been. Had I not ever been able to have children of my own I'm sure I would've turned out to be a teacher or a nurse. My mother said from the time I was very little I was always taking charge and caring for others.

I was 23 years old when I first became a mother. I loved being pregnant and my body was built for it. My husband and I were living separately at the time I found out I was pregnant, since we had different opinions about commitment. It's not that he didn't love me, because I knew that he did, but he was very indecisive about what he wanted in life. I never wondered if he was going to be involved. Turns out that 40 years later we are still together.

I felt I wasn't immediately accepted when I became pregnant with his child. I may not have been considered *bride material.* I got pregnant before marriage, was a little wild, and not traditional in my role as a woman since I couldn't feed forty people with only 15 minutes' notice. I never really felt like I truly belonged in his family and still don't feel like I belong to this day. His mother and I had a wonderful relationship. She was my pillar. I hung on to her some days in my early child-rearing years as she raised 4 boys and a daughter. I'm not sure what I would've done without her help.

Rough, tough, and tumble is the best way to describe my 3 boys. They love horses, hockey and football, hunting and fishing, and fists are not uncommon either. Being in a home with all men is hard. There's a balance to be had. Holding the feminine energy of the home was challenging at times. I'm not a girly-girl myself. It was hard but it was fun as my boys were so full of energy. Some days I would just sit in awe of them and smile to myself as I would watch them play. Kindness and decency were at the forefront of expectations in our home. That covered everything. You treat people the way you want to be treated. Show compassion, love and, gentleness to others until you can't. That's important for every man to understand. I raised my boys in a different world than I grew up in and reminded them of that. I knew they weren't going to have a wife like their mom. I never worked full-time while raising the boys as I just couldn't do it. I always chose a part-time job, which kept me learning, feeling challenged and gave me purpose outside of being a mother.

One of the biggest challenges of having a husband work away from home, was discipline; for both myself and my children. There were times he was working away from home for 6 weeks at a time. We had a wood-burning stove so even getting wood into the house every day was a challenge. I was very stubborn and willful with the boys since I couldn't back down. I didn't have backup! There was hockey and 4H to get them to. I didn't think I'd be able to do it because money was tight. I remember sitting at the kitchen table sorting through the bills as they needed to get paid and deciding that I had to quit smoking for at least two weeks so I could pay the bills. I would stand in line at the grocery store having $150 for two weeks' worth of groceries and decide which groceries to put back if I over-spent.

I remember the one time as a young, tired mom, my youngest was just a baby and I had spent hours doing laundry; ten baskets full I'm sure. The boys were jumping off of the deep freeze into the laundry baskets like superheroes and all of the laundry that I had just spent hours folding was everywhere, and I snapped. Both boys got a spank and thankful for them, their grandmother walked in just at the right time. At that moment I realized that I had to get ahold of myself or I was going to really struggle as a mother.

When I found out I was going to be a grandmother for the first time, my heart dropped a little bit as my son was still only 21 years old and in school and so was his wife. As long as I'm alive I'll always replay this scene in my head. My son came in, popped into bed beside me and said, "Mom, you're going to be a grandma" and my instant reaction was, "Ohhh Ben…" with a slight sigh in my voice as I knew the hardships that would be ahead for them at their young age. His reaction back to me was just as instantaneous. It was full of disappointment and a little anger. He had expected me to be more excited than I was. I know that my response had an impact on our relationship and it broke my heart. I've now had the pleasure of seeing the father he's turned into. He is dedicated to his kids 100% and I couldn't be more proud of him.

My favourite thing about being a grandma is the love I feel for my grandbabies. I never understood the depth of that love when I would hear other grandparents talk about it until I finally understood it. There's something to be said about your child's child because you had a hand in that love. Seeing your own child fall in love, and the culmination of that love in a child is one of the most beautiful things in life if you're fortunate enough to experience it. I don't think that there's a day that goes by that being a grandmother doesn't remind me of being a mother. You're still giving, but it's just a different kind of giving.

When I became a mother, every fibre in my body was dedicated to that job; that's how strong the pull was for me. Like every mother, I would feel my children's pain. It felt so surreal. There were never times that I felt I had a higher calling than being a mother but it was still incredibly difficult. No one has ever been responsible for my happiness but me. I've experienced pain, sorrow, and abuse but it doesn't define who I am. I am so much more than what's happened to me. I've never been a victim in my life, and that's the part of me that my mother gave me. She gave me my "scrap" and my determination.

I hope that I never lose my words and my sense of compassion and empathy. Compassion comes and goes but empathy you have to feel. More than anything I hope I never lose self-compassion. You have to learn where to pick your battles and not stress over the small stuff as a mother. We've all been there. You're not alone, even if you feel like you are. Reach a hand out for help, and another mother will be there to take it. It's our job to keep moving forward and bring everyone along with us.

The Woman in the Mirror

Recently I was invited to present as the keynote speaker at a mental health conference for high school students and it was one of the most powerful moments I've experienced in my teaching and speaking career. Why? Because I cried in front of 150 teenagers.

In preparation for the keynote address, I thought about how I could best relate to teens and their struggles with mental health as a 43-year-old, working mother of four. So, I dug out my high school journal, to revisit my thoughts and feelings as a teen. For first time ever, I shared some of those journal entries publicly, with a gym full of kids.

What I wanted the youth to understand is that what you see in front of you, doesn't always tell you the whole story. The struggles of self-confidence, self-worth, and self-esteem as a teen often follow us into adulthood, and we learn to hide them well. I didn't intend to cry, but as I read through a few of those journal entries, the ones that highlighted my self-doubt, and struggles with my weight and self-esteem, the tears just made a surprise appearance. It was a powerful moment, to cry as a grown woman in a room full of teens, but the most memorable thing from that experience was how those kids held space for me.

They were silent, and patient, as I paused to wait for my emotions to pass so that I could catch my breath and begin speaking again. Then, one teenage boy sitting in the back who must've been about 16 years old, gave me a little encouraging cheer out loud as if to say "we got ya!" Next, a young girl sitting in the front row walked up to me and handed me a Kleenex to catch my tears. Words cannot even describe how I felt at that moment. I was there to support and encourage them, bringing a message of the importance of prioritizing our mental health. What these teenagers didn't know is that they in fact supported me by allowing me to heal as I shared parts of myself.

I've struggled with self-esteem and body image since I was old enough to start comparing myself to the other girls around me. Every time I looked in the mirror I saw someone who wasn't quite good enough. I was too *big* for ballet at the age of six so I quit after my first year. As a young figure skater, my boobs were far too big to feel comfortable in those spandex dresses we had to wear and my thick thighs were sure as hell not wearing those panty shorts that were part of my volleyball uniform so I opted for the longer grey Huskie shorts. *If only I looked like my two best friends growing up, life would've been so much easier.* I would've been able to land my high-school crush. I wouldn't have had to give myself up intimately to the first guy who asked for it. When I read that high school journal prepping for this book I sobbed, I literally cried uncontrollably. The tears were for the teenage girl in me who clearly beat herself up much more than she deserved, and also for the grown woman who still continues to struggle with self-esteem and body image. The tears were for all of the girls and women who are continually trying to love the woman they see in the mirror looking back at them, despite all of their *flaws* and *shortcomings*.

The only time in my life that I didn't struggle with my self-esteem started about seven months after my marriage separation. I had lost about 30 pounds from the *divorce diet* (which mainly meant I wasn't eating) and I was as fit as I'd ever been because I was running. Everything had all fallen apart in my life, yet for once, I had finally felt confident in the skin and body I was in, or at least I thought I did. I wore a size small for the first time ever, bought the cute little shirts and jean shorts I'd always wanted to be able to wear, and finally felt comfortable in a pair of jeans. Yes, I finally rocked a pair of jeans! Yet, I felt more alone than ever and was still trying desperately to save a marriage that couldn't be saved. I got really good at portraying an image in the community that I would be ok, despite all of the soap opera drama that seemed to hover around my divorce.

Throughout the year of my separation and divorce there was one group of special women who were part of my *circle* that helped lift me back up again. Two of them, Carla and Candace, are the sole reasons why I am a BodyTalk practitioner now as they lined up my very first BodyTalk session during an intervention weekend when my mental health had hit an all-time low. I became friends with them a few years prior when I worked in direct sales for a jewelry company called *Lia Sophia*. The women I met in our team group, our sisterhood, were and still continue to be, some of the most inspiring, fun and kick-ass women I've ever met. Another friend, Celena, became one of my best friends, and we worked together in a few direct sales companies following the untimely closing of Lia Sophia. From the time I started writing this book, I knew that I wanted to invite Celena to be part of this collection of motherhood memoirs.

Celena is one of the greatest teachers I know with a soft, open heart for any and all students and she has a fuel and passion in her soul to just make things happen in her life. She's inspired so many women in her journey of direct sales, encouraging women to celebrate their brilliance and beauty. She thrives by challenging and pushing herself to new goals and leads by example. One of the things I love most about her is that she's incredibly funny, and uses humour and her jovial spirit to connect with and lift up others. She makes it her mission to help women feel good about themselves and her words offer inspiration and encouragement when we are hardest on ourselves. I am so thankful that she accepted the invitation to share what journey led her to the path of leading and inspiring women.

Brilliant & Beautiful

CELENA GUNVILLE

As a little girl, I was very independent and mother-like. My dad's relationship with my little brother wasn't the easiest so I always felt incredibly protective of him. I felt it was my responsibility to help keep him out of trouble. I was that keener who always wanted to help and please people. At school I was quiet, shy and sank into the background, desperately wanting to be noticed by somebody. I never felt unloved at home, but I still wanted to be noticed.

I am of mixed blood but registered status First Nations. My father is Cree and my mother is French but because they got married when the Canadian Government was working through reconciliation for First Nations people, my mom did receive Treaty status. There was no Cree spoken or Indigenous culture traditions growing up for me. If anything, we celebrated mom's French heritage as we attended French Immersion school as kids. Growing up going to an "elite" French Immersion school with a last name of Bear presented some challenges for me. For the most part, all of the other children were white. I didn't have the name brand clothes they did and I just felt different, because I was different.

In Grade 3 I hosted a birthday party, and all of my friends from school came just as I would've gone to their parties. I got to school one day after the party and received a note from one of the girls. She said it was from her mom. The note was asking for all of their birthday gifts they had given me back. I looked at the note and knew damn well her mom didn't write it. The note also said that the girls couldn't be friends with me anymore because my last name was Bear. I was so ashamed, I didn't tell anybody about it. I did bring all of their gifts back to school the very next day. I could not wait until I got married so my last name wasn't Bear anymore.

I ended up having no friends for the rest of the school year. If I think about who my friends were after that I honestly think that I actually didn't have any friends until my Grade 8 year. I had no one to play with during recess or lunch and stood by the door alone all by myself. I wasn't even that kid that tried to walk with teachers. It bothers me now as a teacher that no teachers ever asked me to walk with them at recess or stopped and asked if I was ok. Where were they? They had to have seen that I was by myself and alone. I just wanted someone to notice me.

I was in the resource room as a kid because I had trouble reading. Math came easy to me, but I wasn't a student that everything came easy to. Now, as a teacher, I am passionate about reaching and supporting all learners because I was *that kid* growing up in school. I really believe that some teachers never had to be a *student*; things just came easy to them. They never had to struggle with learning or making friends. I think that teachers who struggle with connection in the classroom or find it difficult for students to know, like, and trust them all goes back to their own experiences as a child and students.

When I was 12 years old, my mother encouraged my dad to move us onto the reserve at Muskoday. Mom's thoughts were that it would allow us to be closer to dad's family and we could connect better with our Native roots and heritage. Dad was hesitant but we did end up moving there for a few years. I still felt the line of division between me and the other kids. I feel like I didn't fit in either at the reserve or at the French Immersion school that I was still attending.

I went to a few Pow Wows when I lived out on the Reserve, but as a Grade 8 girl who was fairly pretty, I was always being threatened by other girls, so I just stopped going. I would be asked out by the guys, so the girls would hate me. I wasn't a fighter, but those years and experiences definitely turned me into thinking I was a fighter. It became really hard living out there, and I found it much easier to befriend boys than girls. The guy friends I had were the ones who brought me into the circle of friends out there. In the end, the girls became my friends and weren't threatened by my existence.

I always knew I wanted to be a mother from the time I was just little. I would practice breastfeeding and putting my doll to sleep. I thought I would be pregnant and married at 19 years old. Lo and behold, I was pregnant at 16 years old - but it certainly wasn't planned. I felt like I became another First Nations teenage statistic. That fired me up to be not dependent on the system and my thoughts were, "I'm old enough to have sex, I'm old enough to deal with the consequences."

I was so insecure as a teenage girl and had a boyfriend whom I wanted very much to like me, and as it goes with many teenagers, I had sex with him when I didn't even want to. Once I found out that I was pregnant I instantly got rid of him because I knew he wasn't good for me, nor would he be good for my child either. I knew that I would go ahead with the pregnancy since I was 110% against abortion at that time.

After I had Jada I became a bit of a hermit as my entire life was work, school, and my daughter. I would go to school, leave for home on my spares to nurse her, go back to school, come home and nurse her again after school and then go to work. Mom would bring me her on my break at work so I could nurse her again. Thankfully I had supportive parents because at that time there was no daycare at the high school. The downfall of young motherhood is that I didn't recognize that I was growing up with her as I raised her.

As a young mother, I was independent and met both of our needs with no issues at all, but looking back now I realize Jada was always along for the ride and never on the pedestal. I was falling in love with her beside me, getting married with her beside me. I was still selfish as a 17-year-old and that's where some of my regrets lie. I'll fight tooth and nail to say that I was a good mom to her, but I will also be the first to say that I wasn't a good mom.

At 19, I was going into my second year of University and had a mutual *hook-up* with a friend. Lord love a duck, I got pregnant again. Jada and I were already living on our own and I knew I wasn't going to ever be with this guy in the future. I was a single mom, on my own, and had to really dig deep and reflect on how this pregnancy would affect both Jada and me. I came to the realization that I could not have that baby, so I made the decision to have an abortion. I ended up telling my Grandma, who I was very close with and she told me to not dwell or worry on that decision as it was the best decision for me and Jada at that time. It never ever crossed my mind after that to judge myself for that decision even though I was 110% against abortion before. I decided after that, "No more sex, Celena." I wasn't going to go on birth control to have random sex.

The mother-daughter relationship that Jada and I had and continue to have can be challenging at times. She became very independent herself as a young child. She'd watch her Disney movies all by herself in her room just fine. She didn't need me. She definitely got her independence from her mama. When she was seven years old she went from being an only child to the middle child as I had married my husband Trevor. We had a son together and his older child (my stepson) moved in with us too. Jada rarely heard the word *No* from me and when it started to happen into her teenage years, there became a power struggle between the two of us.

Looking back at those years of raising her I realize that there were so many things we could've done differently - as most mothers do. We allowed her to check out. We lost her to her phone and allowed her to spend endless hours by herself in her room. We didn't push for her to spend time with us, not even meals. She was so independent, but I do wish we would've made a point to engage her more often as maybe our relationship would be different.

I believe that I'm reconnecting now to my culture in my own ways. The reconnecting started when I attended Saskatchewan Urban Native Teacher Education Program (SUNTEP) at the University of Saskatchewan to get my education degree and it was steeped in holistic approaches to teaching and learning. It was a mixture of experimental learning, theory, and lecture. I attended sweat and culture camps and began to immerse myself more and more in the Indigenous experience. As a teacher in a school that was almost all First Nations students, I continued to learn and grow as I connected with my culture and heritage. I worked on a three-year Aboriginal Integration project integrating Aboriginal content and resources using the curriculum. Eventually, I took on a position with the Saskatchewan Ministry of Education in a program called *Following Their Voices* and had the opportunity to meet and learn from Elders, Indigenous youth, and families. The sequence of events in my life led me back to the reserve I lived on as a teenager, and as a teacher there now, I'm continuing to learn about cultural ceremonies and getting the opportunity to know more about my own family tree and build relationships with those family members.

Teachers spend more hours of a day with students than the parents of those children and I feel not all teachers may realize the profound impact that they have on students. I can reflect now on my earlier teaching days and realize that I did have *favorites* in the classroom. Some of the work I did for the province in the *Following their Voices* program opened my eyes to the importance of acknowledgement of every, single student. When you're a teacher, every child in your classroom has to be your favourite in some way. Every child in your class needs to feel like they matter to you and that they feel welcomed. I did not feel like that as a student.

Years ago I started doing some side work in the direct sales industry and it's been incredibly life-changing for me. My side hustle of selling jewelry has really helped me find my confidence back. I was good at sales without even trying to be good at it, because I was passionate about helping women feel brilliant and beautiful with just one piece of jewelry. Wearing jewelry always makes me look good, feel good, and feel special. The bonus is that jewelry always fits, no matter what. Today, I'm the heaviest I've ever been, but part of me also believes I'm the most beautiful I've ever been. I really believe it's the sisterhood of the company I work with, Plunder Jewelry, that has given me that sparkle back in my eye and the pep in my step. It's beyond anything I've ever experienced before. The things that other women do for one another to support and encourage them within the company are so uplifting and an amazing culture to be a part of. Every woman should experience that kind of connection and support from other women as many of us struggle to feel like we fit in and belong.

During the midst of the Covid19 pandemic, I had a *Who am I?* moment where I felt lost and struggled with my mental health as I felt disconnected. I know that when I take care of myself, I can better take care of those I love. I sat down with myself and the four aspects of whole health from my Indigenous culture; mental, emotional, physical and spiritual self. I challenged myself to reflect on what it is that I actually want. What is it that I wish for? What do I want to learn more about? I made a goal to focus on my jewelry business as it always fueled my soul. I began to move my body more and spend more time in nature. I can still listen to my podcasts or be on my zoom meetings while being outside. I immersed myself more in continuing to learn about my Indigenous culture and history. I challenged my creative mind by refinishing furniture and other creative projects. I started listening to music during mundane activities like mopping my floors as it brought me so much more joy.

What I've realized about myself is that like most women, I tend to fall into patterns of starting and stopping things; especially when it comes to my health. As soon as I find myself trying to lose weight I tend to self-sabotage. If I take a different approach to weight loss, and look at it from a healthy lifestyle perspective, I feel less pressured and more inclined to do the work.

To be whole you must connect with the four parts of self - mental, emotional, physical and spiritual. You must know what it is that *you* truly want, wish for and hope for; not just for your family, but for you. When you feel whole, you'll experience more love for yourself which will pour over into those you love more effortlessly. When in doubt, rock a beautiful piece of jewelry and step into your brilliance and beauty.

Good Mother

The truth about pain is that it's super tricky to hide. Even those of us who have become masters at stuffing it so deep no one will ever find it again, pain always finds a way to peek out. It also always finds a way to hide out in the body until we begin to listen closely. If you are perceptive enough you may be really good at seeing and sensing where people carry their pain. It's in their eyes and in the way their shoulders slump so as to protect their heart. It's in their gait and the intonation in their voice. You can sense it in their energetic field. You can literally feel people's pain if you tune in closely enough.

Grief is a pain that is heavy and burdensome, and one that does not come with instructions or a navigation manual. It comes in all shapes, sizes and forms. How does someone who buries a child experience and process grief differently from someone who loses a grandparent? If your sibling dies by suicide, how does your grief differ from that of your parents? If you become widowed, is your grief different from that of the parents of your beloved spouse? Pain is pain. The way we all process pain and grief can be very different.

I remember overhearing a conversation one day about a woman named Gwen whom I knew that was experiencing unimaginable loss and heartache. In that conversation, I noticed the statement, "If she were a good mother, this may have never happened." It felt ugly to hear and I thought about how many times I felt that same feeling about myself. If I was a *good mother* I never would have...(insert almost any judgement you can think of.)

The gossip mill is always a busy place and unfortunately, word travels fast - whether it be the truth or not. I got to experience this phenomenon firsthand following my divorce. Someone always knew something about me that I didn't. It's an awful feeling to know that people are talking about you and you cannot control what they say. Those looks you get in the grocery store or the side conversations that you are most definitely convinced are all about you, can eat you up inside. All any of us really want is to be loved, accepted and understood. We all make mistakes, and I've yet to meet a mother who isn't harder on herself than those around her are. The thing is, we can never seek to understand from a place of judgement, only from a place of empathy, and empathy requires understanding.

I first knew Gwen back when I was a high school teacher and I taught both of her children. I didn't *really* know her until the day she walked into my office, but I had certainly heard a few things about her. You know how that goes in small towns. I received a text from a mutual friend asking if I would agree to see Gwen for a BodyTalk session as she was going through an extremely traumatic event in her life and was grief-stricken.

I will never forget the day Gwen walked into my office. It was one of the most gut-wrenching days I've ever experienced as a practitioner. I had rehearsed what I would say to her and how I would say it. I thought about what the best way to act and react would be. The hardest part is that I couldn't really do anything but hold space and observe (oh and cry - I cried so much.) We always want to fix and solve as women don't we? It's like if we can't do something at the moment to help ease someone else's pain we aren't worth a damn thing to them. Often the best, and the only thing we can do is be there to be present and listen and so I did just that. Gwen continued to come for regular sessions and during her healing journey, I really got to know the story behind the story.

I invited Gwen as a guest to share her story publicly for the first time on the *Strong as a Mother* series. When life threw her a wrecking ball that demolished her entire world as she knew it, she had a choice to be swallowed up by it or find the tiny rays of hope and healing that peeked through the darkness. As I watched her bravely share some of her most vulnerable pieces of herself and her life with complete strangers that night I choked back tears as I knew this was just the beginning of her sharing her light and hope with others.

C.a.m.

GWEN SINCLAIR

I don't believe there's any perfect mother, we all make mistakes, but I was a damn good mom - before my addiction. I was present, I had patience and I did things with my kids, but when my addiction took over my life it consumed me, and I lost *Gwen*. I couldn't be there for myself, so I couldn't be there for my kids as much as I wish I would've been. All of my priorities were gone. It's like nothing else mattered. I missed so many soccer and basketball games. My addiction hurt them in every single way and took away the mom that they knew.

My daughter, Millisa had eleven years with me as a sober mom. My son Cameron didn't have that. He was 6 years old when I started drinking. He found it hard to remember the *sober mom*, and the experiences we had as a family when I wasn't drinking. All he really remembered was the *addicted mom*.

The early days of motherhood, before my addiction, weren't easy for me. I had always wanted to be a young mom. My dream was to have 6 to 8 kids by the time I was in my mid-twenties and then my family would be complete. It seemed like it would be a really easy job being a mom, but I quickly found out it was a hundred times harder to be a mom than I had thought.

I got pregnant when I was 16 and had my daughter, at 17. The pregnancy wasn't planned but it was the best surprise I've ever received in my life, and I often remind her of that. I think I did well at that age since I was just a child myself really. When it went around town that I was pregnant it wasn't easy. People talked and I was angry at what they were saying. I had actually decided to drop out of school and got myself a job babysitting.

I was so young when I had my daughter, so I had quite a bit of energy and would do *kid stuff* with her. I was really fortunate because my parents supported me and allowed me to still experience being a kid on the weekends. They would let me choose Friday or Saturday night to be with my friends and they kept her with them. They loved being grandparents.

When my second child, Cameron, came along, I was only 22 years old and was working two jobs so I had less time to spend with him. I was lucky because my son's dad had a good job and worked so when Cameron was about a year old I didn't have to work full-time. My marriage to him ended though when Cameron was 4 years old.

After the divorce, I was single for a while, but met and fell in love with somebody at the age of 27. We started spending time together and there always seemed to be alcohol around. Without even realizing it, I would grab a drink here and there because it was always around me. I never imagined that picking up a drink here and there would turn into a full-blown addiction.

Within the first eight years we were together alcohol became part of our story that brought with it so many problems in the relationship. I vividly remember an argument we had on Christmas Day one year. It was a random fight that happened, and he kicked the kids and me out of the house. We were only apart for four months and I have no idea how or why we got back together, but nothing was the same after that.

By the time I was 30, the addiction had completely taken over my life. More often than not I would wake up in the morning and instead of reaching for a coffee, I would be having a drink. It was completely normal for me to feel like I had to drink throughout the day and night. It got so bad that I would go to sleep or pass out, and then get up at 2 or 3 in the morning and have to feed the addiction again. Before I knew it, the addiction took over my identity, and I lost the

Gwen that I was. I lost all of my self-esteem and confidence. Prior to my addiction, I was always a happy, jovial person. I became quiet and didn't really talk to anyone. I was so far into the alcohol that I was lost.

I fully loved him and felt safe with the man I was with, even though I was enveloped by the addiction. I didn't think that I could do life on my own. I was told several times I wouldn't be able to do it on my own. We eventually got married and our marriage was four and a half years long. I'm not sure why we even got married. From the minute we signed the papers, more things seemed to change with us - more distance, more anger, more jealousy. I fell really hard into the alcohol then, buying whiskey in 40 oz bottles and hiding them around the house in every room just to get that one sip in me.

Of course, alcohol abuse affects your health and your looks, and you gain weight. Looking at myself in the mirror I could see the harm that it was doing to me. I would tell myself "This is it. I'm not going to drink." I would last maybe two or three days and then relapse again. I didn't think it was possible to get out of the cycle. I got fed up with being sick and not being able to go to work. I knew other people knew the truth about what was going on. I couldn't face the fact that the marriage was falling apart. I drank more to numb it out because I just couldn't face it. I was 39 when I just had enough and I thought I was doing everything wrong in the marriage. I figured if I got sober everything would be fine, it would fix everything.

I went to detox. I wanted to keep it private but nothing stays private in a small town. I don't know if people really know what detox is but you only stay seven to ten days in detox. If your addiction is just alcohol it's usually seven days, but if it's hard alcohol and drugs, they keep you fourteen days. I stayed for ten days. The rumours that circulated about me were things like "She didn't even last.", "She dropped out.", or "She didn't even finish." I finished it. It was very difficult to know that everyone knew where I was. I wanted to prove them all wrong. I can do this. I can do this marriage. Even if there's alcohol around me I can still do it. I can stay sober.

I stayed sober for eight months which was incredibly hard as everything my husband and I did together involved alcohol. Our basement fridge was right full of a variety of booze, we had a cupboard full of booze too. My husband and I went on an all-inclusive trip to Jamaica with my daughter and her husband; a one-week trip with full access to alcohol. There were so many people that expected me to fall off the wagon. I heard gossip "This is when Gwen's going to drop. She's going to come back as a drunk, again." But I didn't. I stuck to my coffee.

When we got back home, about two weeks later my husband shared with me that he wasn't happy in the relationship and that it would be best if I moved out. I felt my heart break. This was the first relationship that I was in where he made time for my kids and I fully loved him.

The people where I worked started to really support me throughout this time saying "You're sober Gwen, start a new life - you can do this!" That helped my self-esteem and I left still sober but eventually, I couldn't deal with some of the residual pain from the dissolved marriage and I fell off of the wagon. This was my third fall in four years and I started to have thoughts of not wanting to live anymore.

I tried to get sober with detox again and I relapsed. I wrote both of my children *good-bye letters* as I just couldn't do it anymore. I went to the liquor store, bought a big bottle of whiskey and took it home with a plan to drink the entire bottle and not wake up the next day. To this day, I don't know how, besides a guardian angel watching over me, but my son showed up at my house five minutes after I walked in. He didn't know why he came home early from university that day but because he did, I couldn't follow through with my plan. He sat down with me and we talked, we opened the bottle and I began drinking. I remember the words he spoke to me right before I blacked out - he reminded me how much I have to offer this world and don't even know it.

The next thing I knew I woke up in a stretcher bed with a white curtain pulled around me. There was yelling and screaming around me and when I opened my eyes I didn't know where I was. My son took me to a detox centre and told them that I was at the lowest point ever and that he was scared for my life. I was still intoxicated as I had drank so much. I had nothing with me: no cell phone, no shoes, and no vehicle. He took me there and took all of that away from me so I couldn't leave. I begged him to come get me, promising I would stop drinking, but both of my children had heard that so many times before. He refused to come and get me and said I was staying until I did the program again.

This time they kept me for eight days in detox, a short stay. I felt good, that I got ahold of the addiction again. I didn't feel as confident as when I did it the first time as I had already proven that I failed multiple times before, so there was doubt.

Cameron stayed with me the first few days after I was released. He was so nervous that I would relapse again. We would talk every morning and every night. After a month I was beginning to fear that I didn't think I could do it. I was afraid that I would relapse. I looked into treatment with my doctor and my addiction counsellor but still had to wait one whole month to get help. If I had to wait an entire month, I would relapse I just knew it. I finally went to my addiction counsellor and said, "I either get into treatment now or I'll relapse and I'm done." They had me into treatment within two days.

It's very hard to get into detox and treatment. The cards are stacked against addicts because there's just not enough help. I had to take all of the steps to get to my recovery because I couldn't do it alone. There's often so much shame that people feel when going to detox. Nobody knew when I went this time, only my kids. My daughter had my cell phone and would go on my Facebook to make it look like I was posting and would reply if anyone texted me. I just didn't want anybody gossiping about me like before and I wanted to be able to tell my story before anybody could tell it for me.

When I was done with all the steps to recovery, I knew that something was completely different in me the day I drove away from there. I knew that after all, I had gone through, there was no way in hell I was going back there again. It was such hard work, *really hard work.*

During my sobriety, the only people who said they were proud of me or believed in me were my two children. It was the fuel I needed to continue to stay sober. I do wish that other people who loved me could've celebrated my sobriety with me and acknowledged the hard work it took to get there. It seems that other people almost like to see you suffer and then when you start to feel happiness and joy they can't be happy for you and they're not there for you.

I watched my son begin to really struggle with alcohol when he was 19 years old. Prior to me getting sober, we had both tried to quit drinking together a few times. I remember Christmas Eve 2018 he was sitting on his bed crying with a bottle of vodka between his legs. He was sobbing and said to me, "I don't want to be in this world anymore. It's too hard." He had tried detox eight months earlier and failed so I knew he was really struggling but didn't realize how much.

The day of Friday, December 13th, 2019 Cameron called me, distraught that his truck had broken down and it was just one more thing that had gone wrong in his life. I called and talked with him through text messaging at 8 pm that night. I woke up at 5:30 am the next morning to a Facebook message from him that said *"Goodbye"* and that he loved me and was sorry. I honestly felt like he was playing a terrible prank on me because he was always a jokester. I tried to call his phone several times and continuously sent him text messages. His dad and I were texting back and forth because we had both received the same message and were very concerned for him.

I remember texting everyone I could to go look for him. I thought of getting into my jeep but I was literally so panicked I just froze. I was sitting on my couch messaging Cameron when I heard a door slam outside and I ran to my front door. When I opened it, I saw that it was my son's roommate's mother, Diane. I started running back into my house saying, "I don't want to hear it." She told me to get dressed so we could leave for Saskatoon, but I had no control over my body. She went for gas and came back to get me. She knocked on my door, walked in, and wrapped her arms around me. I felt my entire body go weak as I knew she was going to deliver horrible news. She did deliver the worst news a mother could ever hear. She told me that my son was gone. I screamed and peed my pants in shock and horror. I told her to leave and asked her to go tell my daughter and my parents but to tell them to stay away from me. I needed to be alone.

I couldn't believe he was gone. He was such a jokester and I actually believed that it was a terrible joke. It couldn't be real. I just didn't believe it. People were coming to my house bringing me food, and asking me questions and I didn't understand why. To me, it just wasn't real. I was in so much shock. I wasn't able to see his body for 3 days so

I just couldn't believe this was happening. If I couldn't see it with my own eyes, it wasn't actually happening. I felt like everyone around me was losing it.

It was a Tuesday when I went to the funeral home and they had him ready for us to view. We had picked out the coffin; his dad, I, his uncle and his sister. Even after all of those funeral arrangements I still didn't believe it. I remember telling the gentleman who worked at the funeral home that I was scared to go in there and see him because I didn't know what my body was going to do. He let me take the furthest door away so I had processing time. I walked in and I could see the rim of his hat from the back as I walked a little closer I noticed his nose and some of his side features and I knew instantly it was him. I began to run up to him and remember putting my arm around him, crying and saying, "Cameron, what did you do to yourself?" It was an angry sadness with shock and disbelief. I functioned like he was supposed to answer me - like he would sit up and answer me.

I spent four days from noon until night at the funeral home beside him. I couldn't leave him and felt better there by his side. I made sure that his clothing was all on right. I wanted to move him, to hold him, but I didn't want to *hurt* him. I asked the funeral workers to show me how to move him without *hurting* him. I recall the look they gave me as if I was crazy. They showed me how to pick up his hand, and move his arm and I kept asking them, "Are you sure I'm not going to hurt him?" I held him for four days before I had to let him go.

I still go to that place in my mind where I'm expecting him to come back even though I realize he's gone. I do believe in the afterlife and feel him around me. Although I won't have him in this life physically with me any longer, in the afterlife of eternity he is going to see me come in as a little old lady and I'm going to see him as my 21-year-old son waiting for me. I absolutely believe that. I have to believe that to get through each day, I will see him again.

Cameron saved my life but couldn't save his own. That won't ever leave my mind. With all of the words of encouragement that he gave me, how is it possible that he couldn't know that about himself? The *why* will always be there for all those who loved him. We will never know in this lifetime *why*. When I think about everything that he was struggling with I can guess it was an overload of everything he was trying to process in his life. It was just too late.

Anybody that is able to take their own life is struggling with mental health or mental illness. He was battling with alcohol addiction and was so hard on himself. He wanted things to happen too fast in his life. He never gave himself enough credit for all that he had accomplished in his young life. A month prior to his death, he told me he wanted to get help because he saw the difference it made in my life. He just wanted to be happy like me. He reached out to me at the beginning of December to go into detox and asked me to book him in. He was booked in for December 14th and that's the morning he died. It was two days before he took his own life that he told me to call back and cancel his spot because he decided not to go. He was feeling better. I called them to give up his spot.

I wonder to this day, and will forever wonder if there had been immediate help when we asked for it, what a difference it could've made for him. If they would've taken him into detox the day I called, would my son still be here today? Nobody knows that, but he would've at least gotten the chance.

Staying sober through grieving the loss of my son wasn't an easy task. That entire month after he died I don't think alcohol even crossed my mind once because I was in such a state of shock. I have very little recollection of those first few weeks. I was literally a zombie walking around in a state of numbness. When it did start to cross my mind a few months later, I kept telling myself I wouldn't be able to make it through grieving his death if I went back to drinking. I knew my life would be over. Cameron worked so hard to get me sober, and leave me at that detox centre that I wanted to stay solid in my sobriety, living for both of us, for my daughter and grand-babies. I just knew if I went back to alcohol I would die.

I was so lucky that I had my daughter throughout the grieving process, we had each other. By some miracle, on my bad days, she could be there for me and on her bad days, I could be there for her. For some reason, it still works out that way, when one of our strengths drops, the other one is right there for the other. We take turns being the emotional anchor.

When people ask me, "How did you do it Gwen?" I honestly can't answer that question because I'm still doing it, every single day. I still question how I'm doing it. Right now I take life one day at a time but in the beginning, managing the grief was literally one second at a time.

What saved me through addiction was that I started volunteering at detox centres and volunteering my own time to help others who are struggling. I started a Facebook group called "New Hope Comes" for people struggling with addiction of any sort. Being open and honest with my journey has been so healing for me. If I sat back and let the shame of *drunk Gwen* take over, I honestly wouldn't be here today. I am very open and speak honestly about how badly I messed up in life. We cannot go back in time, we can only go forward. We have to accept our mistakes. Everybody makes mistakes and you need to come to terms with those mistakes to make it through.

You can't identify addiction by judging how it *looks*. There are doctors, lawyers, nurses, and people from all walks of life who struggle with addictions. I had so much guilt that my children lost their mother to addiction for over ten years but I always knew that I couldn't go back and change the past. I loved my kids more than I loved myself because I hated who I was. All I could do was just tell them that I loved them and that I was so incredibly sorry for the shitty life I gave them. I had to apologize to my daughter for expecting her to step in and be the mother for her brother when I couldn't. It may still eat me up to this day, but we were able to all sit down and talk about their childhood and resolve so much as I was completely straight and honest with them. Of course, both kids would never be able to escape that part of their lives and neither would I, but it's in the past and all I could really do was show them how much I still loved them.

Three of the people I was in treatment with are already gone, they relapsed and died. It was all set up for me to start volunteering at detox. I needed support when my son died - I needed to talk about addictions. In January and February, I went to meetings and I was set to speak at meetings. Cameron was only gone a month but I needed to speak at meetings. I was denied to go and speak in detox because I was grieving Cameron and they thought I couldn't do it as it was too soon. There was nothing more I needed at that time than to be surrounded by people who would get it, who would get me. I was trying to hold on to my sobriety so hard, but the health district denied me that. To this day, they made the wrong choice, I needed those people in detox. I needed to tell them "Four weeks ago, I lost my child." A year later I was still not allowed to go in and share my story with others because of Covid. I was so angry and hurt. There was nothing more that I needed.

Cameron had no doubt in his mind that I would overcome this addiction. We had a plan on how we would celebrate my one year of sobriety. He was adamant we would do something special together. When the one year came, and he wasn't there to celebrate with me I experienced all of the emotions and that day was so overwhelming for me. I had a tattoo booked but had to be cancelled because of Covid. The day really was bittersweet. Now that I have passed the four-year mark of sobriety it feels normal for me. I'm always going to be an alcoholic but it feels normal to be sober.

Looking back, If I could've done anything different besides not falling so hard into addiction, it would've been to spend more time with my children when they were little. We always think there's going to be tomorrow or the next day, but that's not always promised. I wish I had sat on the floor and played with them more or taken them to the park more. Those are the things I think about. Sometimes we would go to the park for only half an hour because it was scorching hot and I was just tired. It was like, "Ok kids, let's go". They cried because they didn't want to leave and then I'd raise my voice because I was impatient. We are so hard on ourselves as mothers, but we are always trying to do the best we can with the tools we have.

The summer after Cameron passed away I was at the lake with my grandson and there was a black and white butterfly that followed us all over the place. Wherever I was, it would find me. It gave me a very good feeling and I know it was a sign from Cameron. I visit his grave often and I will forever honour him on his birthday, October 4th. That day will always be a day to honour his life, a *Gwen day* with family and friends to celebrate him. His death day is not a day I like to focus on, and not somewhere I like to take my mind, so I choose to anchor to the day he was born. Truthfully, I honour Cameron's memory every single day and will until the day I die.

I recently studied to become a Master Grief Coach and my goal is to work further with it and help others heal through their grief. It's not exclusive just for those who have lost loved ones but it covers grief of all sorts - divorce, career, additions, anything where you've experienced a loss. When I was in treatment, I'll always remember the people who stood up in front of us as living proof that addiction can be beaten if you commit to working on it and never stop working on it. This opportunity gives me the chance to show other people that recovery is possible no matter what you go through. I see a lot of hope and growth in helping others.

For anyone struggling with grief who may need an ear to listen to or a shoulder to lean on please reach out to me at newhopecomes@mail.com. I've started a grief group called C.A.M. in memory of my son. It stands for connections and memories and of course, is his name. I'll always be an alcoholic but now I'm a recovering alcoholic. Grief and my loss of Cameron are much the same. I'm never, ever going to recover from his death. I'll always be grieving the loss of my child. It will always be an emptiness in me but if I can help others going through the loss of a child to see some sort of light, it will help me to survive.

Hope and Courage

About a year after I met with Gwen to do that interview I hosted a *Strong as a Mother* fundraiser for grieving mothers, with author and grief educator, Lisa K. Boehm. Lisa lost her daughter, Katie, in a tragic vehicle accident when Katie was just 17 years old and in her Grade 12 year. By divine design, I met Lisa at a retreat we were both at and we immediately connected on a soul level. Following that retreat, Lisa decided to raise money for the Katie Boehm Memorial Retreat, a healing retreat where *angel moms* would partner with horses at the Empower U Equine Centre (remember Shannon?) to continue their healing journey. I felt a strong pull to help her do that and so invited the *Strong as a Mother* community to be a part of raising money for this worthy cause.

Lisa shared so many profound words that evening with all of the women, highlighting how she continued to live an inspired life after losing her daughter. She reminded us all that we can feel both grief and joy simultaneously and one does not have to diminish or over-shadow the other. She used an analogy of holding your grief in one hand, and your joy in another. What an incredibly powerful visual. She also shared the three things that helped get her through the darkest moments in her life; hope, a tribe of support, and courage. No matter what pain or grief we are carrying, those three things make up the foundation of healing.

Not by coincidence, Gwen, as well as a handful of other angel moms, attended that evening and had the opportunity to meet Lisa. The next day, Lisa texted me as she was wanting to get in touch with Gwen. She felt a calling to invite Gwen to take the final available spot in the Katie Boehm Memorial Retreat for *angel moms*. What a beautiful circle of connection and healing.

Hope and courage are both hard to muster up in dark days but are really the only two things that get us through to the light. Kyla, another mother who sat as a panel guest on the *Strong as a Mother* series, needed both hope and courage to get herself through another dark struggle of motherhood that is often not talked about: chronic and debilitating pain. Kyla's pain was from a reproductive condition that often goes undiagnosed for years in women. In my holistic healthcare practice, I've met many women with endometriosis and their stories all have a common thread: frustration, pain, more frustration, and few answers. Kyla's story of strength and courage is inspiring for anyone navigating mental or physical pain. Her unwavering desire to stay true to her intuition and faith shows us that miracles, in fact, can happen.

It Would Take a Miracle

KYLA TAYLOR

I can't say I ever dreamed about becoming a mother when I was younger. When we were kids, my sister was the one to take interest in playing with dolls and babysitting for the neighbours. I was the one who was always re-arranging furniture in our playroom, so it's no surprise that I ended up owning a decor store later on in life. I really started to think about motherhood more when I was a teenager and started to experience issues with my menstrual cycle. I had pain and excessive bleeding with every period. I would have debilitating pain, but could never really get to the root of what was causing it and why.

I was 21 when I got married and the following year I had exploratory surgery which showed that I had endometriosis. The doctors told me it was horrific and that all of my internal organs were basically glued together. That would explain why going to the bathroom hurt, intercourse hurt, and everything hurt; I was always in pain. I cried and cried at that diagnosis because finally the pain had a name and I wasn't going crazy. I finally thought there was hope.

I felt good for about six months after that surgery but then started to feel awful again. I started seeing different doctors and had another procedure done and felt amazing. I remember both myself and my husband thought I'd finally be good. We went in for the six-week follow up and the doctor looked at me and told me that even with fertility drugs, I had a 1% chance of conceiving and having my own biological children. I felt blindsided and collapsed in the elevator from grief. I had finally felt better than I ever had and we were actually ready to have a baby and now this doctor told us there was basically a zero percent chance.

We were told that if we wanted to have kids, even though there was little to no chance of conceiving, we had to start immediately with fertility drugs. I knew that option wasn't for me, so we decided against it. My husband and I agreed that if we couldn't conceive naturally we would not go the route of fertility drugs or treatments. We believed firmly that if my body couldn't do it naturally, we would adopt. Surprisingly, six weeks later, I was pregnant. This is when my faith in God really grew.

I started to spot and the doctor I saw, told me to go home and come back if the pain was unbearable, because that would mean that I was likely having a miscarriage. I went back the next day and was sent for an ultrasound and it was then recommended that I have a dilation and curettage procedure (D&C). That option didn't feel right to me since I was barely pregnant, had hardly bled and wasn't cramping at all. They urged me again to get the procedure done as they didn't see a yolk sac and didn't believe that the pregnancy was viable. I asked what would happen if I didn't have the procedure, to which they replied they did not recommend going home without it. I followed my gut and left the hospital that day without having the D&C done. I knew somehow that the pregnancy wasn't over and today, my son Lucas, is 19 years old.

One week later I went back for an ultrasound and could see his heartbeat on the screen - I can't imagine if I had followed the advice I was given and had a D&C done. It was a difficult pregnancy and I hemorrhaged when he was born. When he was little we'd ask him, "Hey Lucas, what are you?" and he'd respond, "I'm your miracle, Mama." He knew it. When I'm struggling in life I remind myself that I trusted myself enough to follow that gut instinct when I was pregnant with Lucas and it's never been wrong.

Because of my endometriosis, we doubted we would easily get

pregnant again so we started trying and again, to our surprise, got pregnant quite quickly. Thankfully, our second miracle, Landon, was born healthy and happy. My uterus was worn out by the time he was born and I bled heavily for two years. I was told that if I tried to have another baby again either the baby or I would likely die, so we were done having children. I was 30 years old when the doctors decided to do the hysterectomy that destroyed my entire life.

Due to the severity of the endometriosis and issues with cysts, they cut me open hip to hip to clean everything out as best as they could. After the surgery, I didn't feel right - something was definitely not right. That heaviness and endometrial pain were gone, but I did not feel ok. I was met with a response that suggested it was just my mental health and my own grief about not being able to have any more kids.

I went back to work, still knowing something wasn't right with my body. I kept doctoring and kept being told that the pain was all psychological. It was all in my head they said, but in the process, they removed my appendix thinking that may have been causing the problem. Finally, it was discovered that I had extensive nerve damage as a result of my hysterectomy surgery. The gynecologist that performed my surgery severed seven of the main nerves in my abdomen.

The nerves normally are the size of the width of a strand of hair but one of my main nerves, because of all of this scar tissue and damage, was the width of my thumb. There was not much they could do to repair the damage and so I was put on narcotics for the pain. I went down to the United States for surgery that attempted to repair the nerves. I was in so much pain at that time, my dad had to push me in a wheelchair at the airport.

Following that, I was referred to another neurologist whom I believed to be the one who'd help me. He was much older, therefore, I assumed wiser and more experienced. He put a neurostimulator in my groin to help with the nerve damage, but it wasn't placed correctly and did more damage. I found out afterward that I was the only person in Canada that had ever received this procedure. My doctors in the States said it would be a lawsuit if that happened there.

The doctor told me that there was nothing more that could be done for me and that if I didn't end up in a wheelchair by the time I was 40 years old, it would be a miracle. He urged me to *get my affairs in order* since he didn't think I would survive. I'm sure he thought I was suicidal and if the narcotics didn't kill me, not being able to handle the pain would eventually do me in.

With no hope, I spiralled into a deep depression after that. For six months I didn't get out of bed and didn't talk to anyone. There was one day I tried to numb all my pain and end it by taking a hand full of oxycontin and downing it with vodka. I was so angry at myself because I failed at that attempt. I couldn't even do that right. I didn't want to leave my loved ones, but I just thought I was the biggest burden in everyone's world. It would be done and no one would have to worry or take care of me anymore. I realized after that attempt, I was still meant to be here and would have to fight to figure out what my path to healing would be. Once again, my faith kept me going.

My mother and father came to help with the two boys and my husband was coping the best he could, which wasn't very well. I managed to wean off of all of the narcotics when I went down to the United States. I was addicted to them, whether or not I wanted to admit I was. I remember thinking that taking the oxycontin daily was like drinking a tiny bit of bleach every day - I knew it wouldn't kill me that day, but eventually, it would. I got ulcers on my tongue and it took two years for my taste finally came back. It's just poison. The problem was, the pain was still there, because of the nerve damage.

I had this wonderful specialist in Regina who knew I was in so much pain and asked why I hadn't tried medical cannabis. My response was, "Because my mother told me never to do drugs as a teenager." I never questioned taking oxycontin or other narcotics, but I had this very strong engrained belief system about weed.

I did some research and talked to a neurological pharmacist because I was so scared of being stoned and losing my brain again like I did when I was on narcotics. After the first two weeks of taking marijuana, I could feel the difference. My pain was being managed and my brain was working. It was the first time I ever thought that I just might make it. The crazy thing is I had to jump through so many hoops to get medical cannabis but could get those narcotics with no problem. Prior to going off of the narcotics I was taking 5500 pills a year. The only thing I'm on now is my cannabis oil at night and my heart medication that was caused by all of the stress. I went from not walking on my own well and sleeping in a fetal position from all of the pain to progressing to the point where my physiotherapist had never seen such a great turnaround for mobility.

In the midst of all of this, I was a mother of two small boys. I knew in my heart of hearts that I might not make it. I finally had these miracle kids and now couldn't take care of them the way I had anticipated I would. I couldn't be *Supermom*, since I was stuck in bed. So instead, I cuddled, and watched their favourite TV shows, played Lego and knew every character. I prayed with my kids and encouraged them to be polite, kind, and respectful. At one point I had started writing them letters in case I wasn't going to make it but soon realized that if I kept focusing on that, I really wouldn't make it, so I ripped them up. I knew that if I only had so much time and did my best to raise the best boys I could, they would be okay whether or not I was alive or gone. There was a true fear that they would lose me but they didn't use that fear to rebel. Instead, they used it to be kinder, gentler human beings. I needed them as much as they needed me. If I didn't have my kids, I wouldn't have survived that time in my life. On the day my oldest son graduated I gave him one of the letters I had written that was supposed to be for him on his graduation day. In tears, I handed it to him, saying I didn't think I was going to make it this far. His response was, "None of us did mom, but here you are."

My boys' father and I divorced years ago but we still co-parent well together. He will always be the father of my children and I care about his well-being. I don't think I ever thought about how hard my illness was on him until after I got through the worst of it. Watching your wife in so much pain and worrying whether or not she would live or die couldn't have been easy.

There is such a stigma and lack of understanding and empathy for people who suffer from chronic pain. I had someone quite close to me, whom I had great respect for prior, tell me that I was just depressed. He told me that I needed to get out of the house and go for a walk. He handed me a book, said he was praying for me, and shut the door and left. Had he approached that situation differently and offered to walk with me, and help me so I wouldn't fall, or come and visit me, it may have been helpful to me. Years later I approached him and told him that his actions and words made me feel judged.

Owning my flower shop business, Daisies, Dreams & Decor, has given me the opportunity to connect and hold space for others who are also struggling. It's a space that makes people feel warm and welcome and that might offer them hope, healing and connection. Creating funeral arrangements for loved ones is something I am passionate about. It's the last beautiful tribute to a loved one and I feel so honoured to be part of that process with families. I make it a point to add unique, special touches to the arrangements of loved ones so that the families feel very connected to them through the flower arrangements.

I didn't share my story for so long because I didn't want to say how awful it was. I knew finally that I needed to tell it because even if I just helped one person who also struggles with chronic pain or disease, it would be worth it. I am most proud that I have raised two very good young men and that I didn't succeed in taking my own life at my lowest of lows. I wish I would've valued myself more throughout the process of my illness and not been so hard on myself when I was physically unable to do things I thought I should've been doing. I wish I would've met me today and known that I was going to make it when I was at my worst and had no hope left.

If you're someone who's struggling with your physical or mental health please remember to follow your heart for your own healing, because only you know what you really need. Challenge things that don't feel right, and make the decisions that are best for you, regardless of what others think. Don't worry if your house isn't clean and perfect or if you have to feed your children cereal three times a day some days. It's ok, they won't die. Your loved ones want you there and they can't ever get you back if you don't make it. Simplify your life and find someone who will take some of the burdens off of your shoulders. On the days you think you just can't possibly keep going, know that you can. There are people who love you and will help you. They won't think that you're a failure or that you're weak. Be ok with not being ok all the time.

I was ordering some prints for my shop one day and one particular print stood out to me. It was a ship in still water and a beach with one chair on it. I thought it was so symbolic of my life. Looking back, I realize that I have let others control my life way more than I should've as I've sat stuck and still in the water. As a people pleaser, I've let others adjust my sails and set my course. I have felt my entire life that I haven't been able to sail my ship on my own because others are drilling holes in it, so instead of moving forward, I just stood still. I've learned to kick those off of the ship who were drilling the holes. I can invite people back onto my ship but it's up to me who comes on and how long they stay. I'm not going backwards anymore or my boat isn't going to sink. I'm ready to sail forward into what's next for me.

I am grateful for all of the lessons I have learned and continue to learn on this journey of motherhood, but I'm most grateful for my amazing two miracle boys. They've always kept me going and still do. They are wonderful young men and I am blessed to be their mama.

Love and Pain

At some point in our lives, every one of us will, without a doubt, experience two things; love and pain. Connection is the common thread that binds humanity and is the tie that binds both love and pain. Without connection we can quickly lose our way, mentally, emotionally, physically, and spiritually. As women, we are especially wired for connection and if our relationships are strong and healthy, then usually, so are we. Finding your *people* can be difficult though and the dynamics of friendships and relationships change and evolve throughout our lives as we change and evolve. We are always becoming new versions of ourselves - every, single, day.

The stories shared in this book tell of struggles that have been experienced by women for centuries. Balancing life with marriage, motherhood, work, life pressures and expectations all while keeping our mental health in check, feels impossible many days, yet we do it.

As I sat with each of the women featured in the book, I felt an overwhelming sense of gratitude and genuine appreciation and respect for them. Their stories represent a collective of women whose stories often go unheard as they strive to be the best the can be for their loved ones with the cards that life has dealt them. I also know there are many, many women in my circle whose stories aren't in this book, but that makes them no less impactful to me and my own journey. I am incredibly grateful for everyone who has shared their story and pieces of themselves with me in my office or in the safe space of the *Strong as a Mother* community.

I've been a mother for seventeen years now. It is and will forever be the longest commitment I will have to anything in my life. I've balanced motherhood through a divorce, a major career change, depression, anxiety, a second marriage, the loss of loved ones, and finding my way back to myself again. It's brought so much love into my life and also brought me some pain to unpack. I'll always be on a path of learning, unlearning and growing as a woman, a wife, and a mother.

I have learned that there are five key lessons in life and most of them, I've learned the hard way:

#1 - It doesn't matter what* they *say, it matters what you know is true for you.

Stay the course of that inner voice that guides you; that is your *true north.* There will be times you question it, are judged for it, and times you may even lose connections and relationships over it. In the end, it's always worth listening to that inner voice. No one is more responsible for your well-being and happiness than you.

#2 - Your voice matters and someone needs to hear what you have to say.

Grow through the discomfort, fear of judgement, and vulnerability that comes with unmuting yourself. As women, we are born into a world that mutes us. So many times in my life I felt like (or was told) I was *too much* or *too opinionated.* Loud, powerful voices of women are rarely met with a warm welcome in workplaces or society in general. The more you speak up, the easier it gets. I've also learned in life, specifically through a painful, public divorce, that you don't have to tell the whole story or provide all of the details of your life for others. It's ok if they don't know everything. It's ok if they don't understand you. It's ok if they get it wrong. Sometimes silence holds the most power.

#3 - When life feels heavy, go back to the basics.
The road back to finding harmony and balance in my life has always been achieved by starting with basic things like getting enough sleep, drinking enough water, and fueling my mind and body with nourishing substances and thoughts. In times of stress, zoom in on the important things in life, and those who love you unconditionally. Taking a break from anything that feels heavy, especially social media, is the best way to lighten an emotional load. Connecting with your breath and consciously breathing throughout your day, will ease tension in both your body and mind.

#4. You're not for everyone.
If the people within your circle don't clap for you, they're not really your people, and that's ok. You don't need everyone. You just need a few really good ones, and sometimes it takes a while to find them. Trying to be someone who you are not, just to fit in and be accepted goes against your true integrity and never ends well.

#5 - Big things can be accomplished in a series of small steps.
When we are faced with a mountain ahead of us, whether it be with our physical or mental health, the hardest part of the climb is just really starting it. '*One foot in front of the other*' was my mantra when I ran my half marathon and I tend to tackle life that way too. The path you've mapped out to get up the mountain may not be the best path for you and it might turn out that it's the longest, most arduous path that takes you to where you truly belong.

I have no idea what's in store for tomorrow, next week, or this next year for me or my family, but I do know that I love them fiercely. I will continue to make mistakes, have bad days (or weeks) and get drawn back into the trauma and drama of my past if I'm not taking care of myself. I value keeping up with my mental health maintenance. It's an act of self-love to continue to make it a priority. When I stumble, with the help of my circle of support people, I'll pick myself back up again.

As you close the pages of this book, my hope is that this collection of memoirs and stories finds you where you are in your own healing journey and brings you a warm feeling of connection, healing, and hope. You are not alone in your struggles, even if those around you don't talk about their struggles. In your darkest days, the best thing you can do is just take one step, one moment, one breath at a time. You are worth the love you so freely give to others and on your very worst day, you're still the best in the eyes of those who love you.

Good Karma

Thank you for reading *Behind Closed Doors.*

If you've found this book helpful or inspiring, please let me know by leaving a review. Your honest review will help future readers decide if they would enjoy my book!
A review is the greatest gift you can give an author.
You can go to the book directly on Amazon and leave a review!

Thank you!

About the Author

Laura Lawrence lives in Meskanaw, Saskatchewan with her husband, Alan, and their four children. She is an author, educator, and public speaker who leads with her heart first and leaves a lasting and impactful impression on those she connects with through her authenticity, humour and genuine empathy.

Laura has published three children's books in the niche of mental and emotional wellness and has spoken to and shared her books with thousands of students. Laura's children's books can be purchased by visiting www.lauralawrence.ca/shop.

Download Laura's free mindfulness and meditation resources at www.lauralawrence.ca/resources or book Laura for a speaking event, workshop, or author reading by visiting www.lauralawrence.ca/connect.

Follow Laura on Instagram @authorlauralawrence or on Facebook @Love Bug Books - Laura Lawrence.

As the founder and CEO of Youth Matter Canada, a non-profit organization that supports mental health initiatives and programs for youth, Laura has worked extensively to create impactful programs, events and initiatives to help support youth of all ages. Please visit www.youthmatter.ca for more information.

Manufactured by Amazon.ca
Acheson, AB

13996951R00103